Vegetarians - Godless Heretics?
What vegetarians and meat-eaters alike should know

VEGETARIANS - GODLESS HERETICS?

What vegetarians and meat-eaters
alike should know

Ulrich Seifert

The Word -
The Universal Spirit

Published on December 2013 by:
© *Universal Life*
The Inner Religion
PO Box 3549
Woodbridge, CT 06525
U S A

Licensed edition
translated from the original German title:
"Vegetarier - gottlose Ketzer?
Was Vegetarier und Fleischesser
gleichermaßen wissen sollten"
Order No. S 463 en

From the Universal Life Series with the consent of
© *Gabriele-Verlag Das Wort GmbH*
Max-Braun-Str. 2
97828 Marktheidenfeld/Altfeld, Germany

The German edition is the work of reference for all
questions regarding the meaning of the contents
All rights reserved

Printed by: Klar Druck GmbH, Marktheidenfeld, Germany

Photo credits:
Front Cover: Top: Spring Lambs © Rufoto/fotolia.com;
Bottom: Painting by Francisco Zurbarán:
© Museo Nacional del Prado - Madrid
p. 82 © Stephan Böckling
p. 85 © Volker Skibbe/fotolia.com, p. 87 © sci/fotolia.com,
p. 93 above © cmon/fotolia.com,
p. 93 below © Siegfried Schnepf/fotolia.com,
p. 99 © Firma V/fotolia.com, p. 136 © diegezeiten/fotolia.com
Pages 57, 70, 77, 78, 91, 99 Archive Gabriele-Verlag Das Wort

ISBN 978-1-890841-48-5

*For the animals,
our fellow creatures
from the hands of God*

The Hope of the Animals

*And I will make for them a covenant on that day
with the beasts of the field, the birds of the heavens,
and the creeping things of the ground.
And I will abolish the bow, the sword,
and war from the land,
and I will make you lie down in safety.*
                                        (Hosea 2:18)

*The wolf shall dwell with the lamb,
and the leopard shall lie down with the young goat,
and the calf and the lion and the fattened calf together;
and a little child shall lead them.
The cow and the bear shall graze;
their young shall lie down together;
and the lion shall eat straw like the ox.
The nursing child shall play over the hole of the cobra,
and the weaned child shall put his hand on the adder's
den.
They shall not hurt or destroy in all my holy mountain;
for the earth shall be full of the knowledge of the* L ORD
as the waters cover the sea. (Is: 11:6-9)

Table of Contents

Foreword 13

There's a war raging against the animals 17

The twisting and falsification of the Ten Commandments of God and the teachings of the Sermon on the Mount by the caste of priests changes nothing about their validity! 21

The slaughter of animals was and is an abomination to God and has nothing to do with true Christianity! 26

The followers of Jesus of Nazareth in the first communities were vegetarians 29

The Doctor of the Church Jerome spoke *against* eating animal flesh 32

The prophets of God and Jesus of Nazareth spoke *against* eating animal flesh 33

The caste of priests teaches the opposite of what God spoke through His prophets, and disregards what Jesus of Nazareth taught 37

The Doctor of the Church Augustine, the "archetype of all the Inquisitors dripping with blood": a "friend" of Joseph Ratzinger 41

Jesus, the Christ – according to the Doctor of the Church Augustine – also a "godless heretic" 43

The cynical theories of the Doctor of the Church Thomas of Aquinas: Animals are destined for use 47

Concepts and opinions in church doctrine academically disproved long ago are still considered to be the measure of all things **50**

Anyone who contradicts is eternally damned 53

Animal testing: Unimaginable cruelty blessed by the Church 55

Animal protectors and vegetarian are "heretics" – eternally damned by the Church 58

"She [the Church] must therefore with painstaking care, remove and eradicate anything that is contrary to faith ..." 61

Upright followers of Christ, yes, entire Christian communities of faith, were bloodily persecuted by the Church 62

Emperor Constantine turned Christianity into a state religion – the fight against the peace-loving vegetarian followers of Jesus of Nazareth became even more brutal 65

Heretics were condemned to death by the Church.
The distinguishing characteristic of a heretic:
He is vegetarian 68

Millionfold and billionfold:
Horror under the guise of ″Christian″ 71

Do not eat the suffering of the animals! 74

The origin of the millionfold suffering of the
animals: Church law 75

The hunt: Torture and death blessed by priests 76

Factory farming: Suffering and misery
blessed by the Church 79

The oceans are being fished empty 83

Fish are also sentient beings! 84

Animal massacre: Condoned by high-ranking
church functionaries 86

Did Jesus of Nazareth eat meat and fish? 94

The unimaginable horror in the barns
and slaughterhouses 100

Catholic and Protestant-Lutheran: Mockery and
derision of Jesus and of His teaching *for* the life 110

Great personalities in world history denounce
the murder of animals 113

Mass murder of people, mass murder of animals:
An enormous guilt, measured by the spiritual-
cosmic laws 120

Vegetarians, the "godless heretics" –
still eternally damned by the Church.
Who is the father of lies? 125

The Third World War has already begun.
Where is the way out? 128

End Notes 137

Sources and other informative literature 141

Foreword

How does one feel as a heretic? Ostracized, derided, despised? Only those among today's vegetarians who are somewhat older can still remember the lack of understanding, the suspicion, yes, sometimes even animosity, that confronted them even just a few decades ago when they consistently abstained from meat.

Today the wind has long since turned. Today, vegetarians are no longer "heretics"; instead they personify the new trend. So why keep talking about the past?

Because, at bottom, it is not the past. Because the animals still suffer terribly. Because the cruelty of man against his second neighbor, the animal, is still on the rise. And because hardly anyone even thinks about why this is so. What shapes man's behavior and more or less controls it? Not lastly, religious concepts – or, ethical-moral values, conveyed to us in our parent's home, at school or in church – or not.
Of what use is the trend toward a vegetarian or vegan diet to the pig or cow that right now, at this moment,

is being cut open and skinned while still alive, due to insufficient anesthetization? From the viewpoint of our second neighbor, the animal, the longed-for trend reversal still progresses – in the truest sense of the word – terribly slowly. The expansion of consciousness of their dim-witted and incredibly unfeeling two-legged "big brothers and sisters" is taking an eternity. The "eternal hell," which the priests once invented to keep us people in check – is actually bloody reality here.

But the caste of priests not only established the animal "hell." No, it recruited all the people it could, and still can, bring under its spell as the torture personnel, as under-devils in human form for this operation of hell – from the first animal keeper to the last consumer.

No. The title of this book – and the television programs on which it is based – is by no means a symbolic-allegoric exaggeration. "Vegetarians – Godless Heretics?" is not a provoking ironic hyperbole, oh no. It simply and poignantly describes the viewpoint of the Church until this very day. This is written in its "rules of operation" – and can be read in this book in black on white.

The more we thoroughly investigate here and decide upon it, the more the animals' hope will grow that the trend speed up – and that they finally receive the respect and love due to them as our fellow creatures.

Matthias Holzbauer

There's a war raging against the animals

The world we live in, and as it is presented to us daily in the media, is frequently characterized by crime. This makes headlines; we hear and read about this worldwide in the media – while other atrocities are not even perceived as the brutal crimes that they are: the overexploitation of the Mother Earth, for instance, or the destruction of the Earth's atmosphere that protects us from cosmic radiation, and not to be forgotten, the crimes against animals for the production of meat and furs, in animal experimentation and much more!

People also brush aside these far-reaching offences against animals and nature so casually, because these abominations have been raised into secular legality by a corresponding legislation, that is, they have been raised to secular law and often – what a pinnacle of cynicism! – with the blessing of the churches, foisted onto the all-too-credulous folk as being "pleasing to God."

Let's just consider the animal protection laws. For the animals, they are a pure farce. They serve only to calm the people's conscience, but contribute practically nothing to the protection of animals! As long as animals continue to be treated as they have been up until now, and this, in a society that calls itself "Christian," the so-called animal-protection law is not worth the paper it's written on. And as long as society considers animals to more or less exist – pardon my saying so – solely to be devoured, and the living, animate being in them is not at all perceived or protected, the fellow creature from God, the animal, doesn't have the slightest chance of a worthy life, because the so-called Christian society is mostly lacking a truly ethical and moral education.

Suggestions for laws that are made by animal protection advocates for an improved animal protection fail over and over again, also due to political parties that call themselves "Christian," and which say that the animal protection clause anchored in the Constitution is sufficient. What a mockery, what cynicism, what evidence of spiritual inadequacy is in this attitude, when we consider the millions upon millions of animals that are skinned alive and cut into pieces! Not to mention the often bestial way of keeping animals.

However, to the misery of the animals, representatives of a people with apparently low ethics and morals sit in the parliaments and often bring their

Catholic or Protestant pattern – that is, merely hollow animal-protection clichés – into the debates. But for the animals, these Catholic and Protestant patterns ultimately mean: War against God's creatures, war against the animals!

Anyone who believes that the body of thought in the Catechism has little influence outside the churches should take note of the following quote made by the Catholic member of the Christian Social Union Party in Parliament, Norbert Geis, on May 17, 2002:

"It's no secret that we have long fought against anchoring animal protection in our Constitution … because there were always efforts to give our basic orientation an eco-centric orientation. In our opinion, **man** *is the sole* **legal person** *in our legal system. There has always been an attempt to also grant rights to plants, animals and other elements of creation and to nature as a whole. … According to our understanding, animals are fellow creatures … but not legal persons. In this sense, they are not an individual.*

The animal has no duties toward people. And therefore, it also has no claim on people to be kept in a species-appropriate way. The possible difficulties for economy and research were not the reason for our reluctance.

Rather, it was and is our concern that the human being remain the central point of our Constitution."¹

By the way, Geis, a Catholic, also had bestowed upon him the Pontifical Order of St. Gregory the Great, granted for his zeal in defense of the Catholic religion!
How is this back and forth, how are these clichés, this cold-heartedness, that is expressed here, supposed to help the animals, and deliver them from their millionfold, deplorable, suffering?

Surely within the churches there are also people who respect the animals and nature and are therefore vegetarian, for instance. But as long as the binding doctrinal statements of the churches, which are against nature and the animals, that is, against the life, which is God, continue to exist and as long as people have to believe these binding doctrinal statements, under threat of eternal damnation, the followers of the Nazarene will continue to expose the untruths, the distortions and ill-concealed negativities and to openly speak out the truth.

The twisting and falsification of the Ten Commandments of God and the teachings of the Sermon on the Mount by the caste of priests changes nothing about their validity!

God, the All-Spirit, the All-Intelligence, the Free Spirit, is not secular law, but justice, and His eternally prevailing laws are the ones that ultimately count. "God is not mocked, for whatever a man sows, that he will also reap," this is what is said by Paul in the church Bibles.

All worldly lawmakers as well as all church functionaries will have to experience this spiritual principle at some time or other, many perhaps only as poor souls in the spheres of purification.

Excerpts from the eternally prevailing cosmic laws, which are instructions of life for us human beings, were revealed by God, the Eternal, through His true prophets. Above all, it is the Ten Commandments of God that were revealed through Moses, and the Sermon on the Mount of Jesus of Nazareth, the Christ of God, whose name the worst criminals and despots in politics and church abuse until today for their satanic works.

Ever more people with a historical education – and many people for whom ethical and moral values are not clichés, or foreign words, that is, people with nobility of heart – know, realize and understand that, right from the beginning, the Ten Commandments of God were falsified as desired by the castes of priests of the respective epochs, that they were distorted and adapted according to their politically enforceable claims to power. They interpreted the word of God totally according to their political majorities – which they purchased or extorted – and according to their often despotic addictions, egoistic inclinations, greediness and much, much more.

God, the Eternal, the All-Spirit, whom we call our heavenly Father, who is the Father of love, the free Spirit, the infinite consciousness, did not appoint any priests; He did not want any churches made of stone and did not found any religions, because He is the free Spirit of love and unity of man, nature and animals.
However, the eternal Spirit, God, the universal consciousness, did appoint prophets to reveal His word and His will to the people, and He sent us His Son, Jesus of Nazareth, the Christ of God, who saved all of creation through His Redeemer-deed. HE, Christ, did not speak of churches, dogmas, rites, sacraments, hosts or wafers, caste of priests, sacrificial cults and

other things. On the contrary: During His entire lifetime, He fought against this!
Until today, it is a fact that the teachings of Jesus of Nazareth, the instructions for life of the Son of God for a lawful life on Earth, which are written in His Sermon on the Mount, are, in truth, rejected by the so-called Christian society and the institutional caste of priests; they are interpreted into a distant future and disqualified as being too utopian for this world.

But whether the priests and the "Christian" politicians like it or not, whether their consciousness is too narrow to grasp the cosmic laws or not, whether they, despite knowing better, act against the Christ of God or not: The Sermon on the Mount of Jesus was, and is, the key of the Christ of God to unlock the kingdom of heaven and to let the Kingdom of Peace of Jesus Christ become reality on this Earth.
In the Kingdom of Peace of Jesus Christ, which has been announced and which will come onto a purified Earth through people who fulfill His will, the laws of life in daily life, no more blood will be shed, not that of the animals, either. Nor will there be any stone churches with priests, bishops, cardinals and certainly no pope. This work of man is becoming subject to transformation, as are many other things.

These times are coming to an end; a new era is beginning.

But the Kingdom of Peace of Jesus Christ will not fall from heaven – it will come only through the fulfillment of the teachings of Jesus, the Christ, according to His words at the end of the Sermon on the Mount:

Everyone then who hears these words of mine and does them will be like a wise man who built his house on the rock. And the rain fell, and the floods came, and the winds blew and beat on that house, but it did not fall, because it had been founded on the rock. And everyone who hears these words of mine and does not do them will be like a foolish man who built his house on the sand. And the rain fell, and the floods came, and the winds blew and beat against that house, and it fell, and great was the fall of it.

And when Jesus finished these sayings, the crowds were astonished at his teaching, for he was teaching them as one who had [divine]authority, and not as their scribes. (Mt. 7:24-28)

Concerning this, several thoughts and questions to think about: During these 2000 years, why haven't the churches done what Jesus of Nazareth taught?

Why did they instead persecute, murder, and – often down to the last child – bloodily eradicate all the truly Christian movements, which took the teachings of the Nazarene seriously in their deeds? And, who was it? Who?

Already back then, Jesus, the Christ, spoke the following, and His word holds true in all eternity:
But you are not to be called rabbi, [that is, priest] *for you have one teacher, and you are all brothers. And call no man your father on earth, for you have one Father, who is in heaven.* (Mt. 23:8-9)

Why then, is there a so-called Holy Father in Rome? Who wants this? What's the point of this? What fruits have come of it? Let us look into the world. Let us look very closely! This apparently is the fruits of the externalized churches!

And just as clearly as Jesus, the Christ, spoke against the priests, He also spoke against killing animals. He said:
Verily, I say to you, I Am come into the world in order to put an end to all blood offerings and to the eating of the flesh of animals and birds that are slain by men.

In the beginning, God gave everyone the fruits of the trees and the seeds and the herbs for food; but those who loved themselves more than God or their neighbor corrupted their ways and brought diseases into their bodies and filled the Earth with lust and cruelty. Not by shedding innocent blood, but by living a righteous life, will you find the peace of God.

You call Me the Christ of God and you speak true; for I Am the way, the truth and the life. Walk this way, and you will find God. Seek the truth, and the truth will make you free. (Gospel of the Holy Twelve, Chap. 74:9-12)[2]

The slaughter of animals was and is an abomination to God and has nothing to do with true Christianity!

The falsification of the teachings of Jesus of Nazareth by church functionaries as well as the colossal misguidance of the people, often enforced with stark, bestial violence by state and church, blessed by church laws, have brought the world to the state it is in today.

All the suffering in this world, above all, the immeasurable suffering of the animals, with all its sadistic, that is, satanic, excesses, is very particularly the fault of those who, in reality, are disguised pagan priests, but who call themselves "Christian," and have presided in the institutional churches for centuries, even though, until today, they think that the spiritual teachings of the Nazarene, Jesus, the Christ, are pure utopia.

The suffering in this world is consequently the fault of those who hypocritically pose as "Christian" leading figures and continue to manipulate the people in a way that is contrary to the true Christian teachings, especially as concerns the nourishment of mankind, above all, the eating of animal carcasses, with its devastating effects for the individual person and soul, as well as for all of mankind. Viewed historically, it is nothing more than the old pagan blood cult, the eating of the flesh of animal sacrifices.

The early Christians, however, were pacifists, conscientious objectors, animal protectors and vegetarians. For those who seek historical evidence, there are records that have been passed down. There is an exchange of letters between various historical personages of the first centuries that clearly confirms that eating meat was and is an abomination to God and has nothing, absolutely nothing, to do with Christianity!

With what justification should we still believe all the priests, pastors, bishops and other opinion-makers, who still want to trot out to us all-too-many untruths – including eating meat as allegedly allowed by God? For the dogmas and dogmatic declarations of the churches are the work of man. Jesus, the Christ, did not teach this. Jesus, the Christ, did not found any churches or appoint any priests. Even though the brazen attempt is made in the dogmas to derive claims from Jesus, the Christ – all these turns of speech and partly absurd declarations are the work of man, which have nothing, absolutely nothing, to do with – in appearance – the plain, courageous man, the carpenter from Nazareth, Jesus, the Christ, the Son of God, and His plain and simple teachings of the Sermon on the Mount. He, Christ, spoke plainly and simply: *Follow Me!* Anyone who knows the history of the churches knows that it is anything but the following of Jesus of Nazareth.

The followers of Jesus of Nazareth in the first communities were vegetarians

To better understand these clear statements, some historically documented quotes show how the apostles, the prophets of God and people in the first communities acted regarding the consumption of meat.

Peter stated that he lived on bread and olives, to which he only seldom added a vegetable.
> *The unnatural eating of flesh meats is as polluting as the heathen worship of devils, with its sacrifices and its impure feasts, through participation in it a man becomes a fellow eater with devils.* [3]

The following statement has been passed down about Paul:
> *Jesus instructed me to eat no meat and drink no wine, but only bread, water and fruit, so that I be found pure when he wants to talk with me.* [4]

Clemens of Alexandria writes about Matthew that he
> *lived on seeds, the fruit of trees and vegetables without meat.*

And: *John, who carried temperance to the extreme, ate locust buds and wild honey.*[5]

According to Church historian Hegesipp, John also never ate meat.[6]
James, the brother of the Lord, lived on seeds and plants and touched neither meat nor wine.[7] And according to the authors of the 2nd century, the other apostles and disciples were also vegetarians.

"Doctor of the Church" Quintus Septimius Tertullianus (ca. 150 – 220) is counted among the oldest of the church authors. He divided the Christians into two groups: the "true Christians," who abstain from meat, and the "bodies without souls," who eat meat. Tertullian writes:
Moreover, what folly it is for you to credit with a thirst for human blood the very people on whom you confidently rely to shrink with horror from the blood of cattle … [8]

Basil the Great, Archbishop of Caesarea, also a "Doctor of the Church," passed down the following statement:
As long as one lives moderately, the fortune of the house will multiply. The animals will be safe, no blood

will be shed or animals killed ... The table will be decked solely with fruits given by nature and one will be content with that ...[9]

It is hard for one to love virtue when one is gladdened by meat dishes and festive meals.[10]

Church father, Gregory of Nazianzus, (ca. 330-390) stated:
The indulgence in meat dishes is a disgraceful wrong and I desire that you may strive to offer your soul nourishment that lasts eternally.[11]

John of Antioch, called Chrysostomos (ca. 349-407), reported about a group of Early Christians:
No streams of blood flows at their place; no flesh is slaughtered and cut to pieces ... One does not smell there the awful vapor of meals of meat ...[12]

The Byzantine Governor Pliny the Younger confirmed to his Roman Emperor Trajan in a letter, that the Christians abstain from every kind of meat.[13]

The Doctor of the Church Jerome spoke *against* eating animal flesh

About 1600 years ago, Jerome (347-420) compiled the first comprehensive translation of the Bible (into Latin). He knew that Jesus said not to eat meat. Why did Jerome not include this teaching in the New Testament, even though there are apocryphal writings that unequivocally report about this? Why not? That the followers of the Nazarene were vegetarians made them heretics, a fringe group to be fought against in the eyes of the people among the folk and those in power, who still clung very much to the old customs of blood sacrifice. (So, what is it like today?) Jerome would have had to fear for his life if he had truthfully included the crimes against animals in the Bible.

However, in a treatise Jerome, the translator of the Bible, wrote the following:

The eating of flesh was unknown until the deluge. But after the deluge ... the poison of flesh-meat was offered to our teeth ... But once Christ has come in the end of time and Omega passed into Alpha and turned the end into the beginning ... we are no longer allowed ..., nor do we eat flesh ...[14]

Thus far, the "Church Father," Jerome, who is, in addition, venerated by the Church as a so-called "saint." Why don't the leading figures of the Church follow the statements of their own saints? Why aren't the high ethical and moral values of the so-called saints found in the catechisms and church laws, instead of being hidden in less official correspondence?

**The prophets of God
and Jesus of Nazareth spoke *against*
eating animal flesh**

The books of Moses still contain original truths. In Genesis 1:29-31, we read the following:
And God said: "Behold, I have given you every plant yielding seed that is on the face of all the earth, and every tree with seed in its fruit. You shall have them for food.
And to every beast of the earth and to every bird of the heavens and to everything that creeps on the earth, everything that has the breath of life, I have given every green plant for food." And it was so. And God saw everything he had made, and behold, it was very good.

Therefore the appeal: ***Eat no meat!! Do not eat the suffering of the animals!*** Eating meat is truly against the law of life, which is God.

Why do the church dignitaries, the bishops and other leading figures of the churches not keep to what the apostles and their own so-called saints teach? Why not keep to what their own Bible, as the allegedly unadulterated word of God, commands the people, including the leading figures of the Church, the priests, bishops, cardinals and popes, who, after all, should be role models?

Why do the so-called ecclesiastical dignitaries speak and live exactly the opposite of what their duty would be, and teach the people against the instructions of God through prophets? Why? Is that Christian – or Catholic and Protestant?

In the Old Testament we can read more clear statements against eating meat. God spoke through the great prophet Isaiah:

He who slaughters an ox is like one who kills a man; he who sacrifices a lamb, like one who breaks a dog's neck; he who presents a grain offering, like one who offers pig's blood; he who makes a memorial offering of frankincense, like one who blesses an idol. (66:3)

And in another passage, God reveals through his prophet Isaiah:

When you spread out your hands, I will hide my eyes from you; even though you make many prayers, I will not listen; your hands are full of blood. Wash yourselves; make yourselves clean; remove the evil of your deeds from before my eyes; cease to do evil, learn to do good; seek justice, correct oppression; ... (1:15-17)

Another passage with the word of God revealed through Isaiah reads:

What to me is the multitude of your sacrifices? says the LORD; I have had enough of burnt offerings of rams and the fat of well-fed beasts; I do not delight in the blood of bulls, or of lambs, or of goats. When you come to appear before me, who has required this from your hand ...? (1:11-12, New KJV)

A justified question: *"...who has required this from your hand ...?"* Wasn't it the priests who required this, who killed the sacrificial animals out of old pagan tradition and burned parts of the carcasses and claimed other parts for their personal carcass meal?

We read further from God's prophet Hosea:

As for my sacrificial offerings, they sacrifice meat and eat it, but the LORD does not accept them. Now he will remember their iniquity and punish their sins. (8:13)

In another passage it says:
For I desire steadfast love and not sacrifice, the knowledge of God rather than burnt offerings. (6:6)

Also through His prophets Micah and Jeremiah, God takes a clear position against the sacrifice of animals. In the book of Job, we find the following statements about nature and the animals:
But ask the beasts, and they will teach you; the birds of the heavens, and they will tell you; or the bushes of the earth, and they will teach you; and the fish of the sea will declare to you. Who among all these does not know that the hand of the LORD has done this? In his hand is the life of every living thing and the breath of all mankind. (12:7-10)

This also describes the experience of many a mystic: And so, everything is animate, everything, also the animals and fish, and the eternal living God speaks through all of life. – He who has ears to hear, let him hear!

Therefore, once more the appeal:
Eat no meat! Do not eat the suffering of the animals!
Eating meat is truly against the law of life, which is God.

All true prophets of God and the apostles spoke against the killing of animals and against eating meat, just like Jesus of Nazareth. His penetrating words are repeated here:

Verily, I say to you, I Am come into the world in order to put an end to all blood offerings and to the eating of the flesh of animals and birds that are slain by men.

The caste of priests teaches the opposite of what God spoke through His prophets, and disregards what Jesus of Nazareth taught

From their own ranks of scribes, presbyters and later bishops, the caste of priests made some into Doctors of the Church and saints, whom they now call "church fathers," and base themselves on their statements. These people, themselves entangled in their all-too-human aspects, allowed the people to continue with the cults of blood sacrifice, as it were, by allowing them to eat meat, because many did not want to leave it.

But until this very day, the vilification of life, the disdain for animals is written in church law. The fact is that through this, nature and, above all, the animals, have to bestially suffer because people's consumption of meat is denominationally and institutionally rubber-stamped. By whom?

When we read excerpts from several doctrinal statements of the Church regarding animals, we learn which forces these churches really serve. We read the following under No. 2417 in the Catholic Catechism:

> *Hence it is legitimate to use animals for food and clothing. They may be domesticated to help man in his work and leisure. Medical and scientific experimentation on animals is a morally acceptable practice if it remains within reasonable limits and contributes to caring for or saving human lives.*

Dear reader, alertness is called for here! Aren't these merely the opinions of priestmen that became church law, priestmen who quite obviously didn't understand anything about God's Creation? Jesus of Nazareth did not teach this. And God, the Eternal, revealed exactly the opposite through His prophetesses and prophets, as has already been, in part, stated.

But let's read on. Under No. 2418, we find:

> *It is contrary to human dignity to cause animals to suffer or die needlessly. It is likewise unworthy to spend money on them that should as a priority go to the relief of human misery. One can love animals; one should not direct to them the affection due only to persons.*

Who determined this? God spoke completely differently through His prophetesses and prophets! And Jesus of Nazareth did not teach this. So, again, only another opinion of priestmen that became church law, priestmen who obviously didn't understand anything about God's creation, meat-eaters who thought of their own stomachs, and nothing else – what else should we call it?

The theologian and religion scholar Prof. Hubertus Mynarek writes in his book: "Papst Entzauberung":

> *Didn't the young theology professor Ratzinger, back then not yet bishop, cardinal or pope, already wholeheartedly emphasize in his lectures before his theology students that nothing better could happen to a deer or*

hare than to be shot and land on people's plates, for with this, the animal would fulfill its destiny, which the Creator-God allotted to it? [15]

That's blasphemy – pure and simple! And a theologian with such life-disdaining views then becomes pope! That is a statement made by the former pope as a young theology professor – but that is solely his opinion, purely a human opinion. Everyone speaks what he is, even Pope Ratzinger.

God spoke exactly the opposite through His prophetesses and prophets. Jesus of Nazareth did not teach this, either. Jesus, the Christ, says:

Verily, I say to you, I Am come into the world in order to put an end to all blood offerings and to the eating of the flesh of animals and birds that are slain by men.

The Doctor of the Church Augustine, the "archetype of all the Inquisitors dripping with blood": a "friend" of Joseph Ratzinger"

In the book written with Peter Seewald "Light of the World," Joseph Ratzinger also gives us insight into his inner life:

But I also invoke the saints. I am friends with Augustine, with Bonaventura, with Thomas of Aquinas. Then one says to such saints also: Help me! [16]

For which values or crimes such alleged "saints" bore witness when they were alive is also found in the centuries-long history of the Church. In his book "Kriminalgeschichte des Christentums" ("The Criminal History of Christianity"), Karlheinz Deschner dedicated a whole chapter to Augustine, and there it says about this "friend" of Ratzinger:

Augustine claimed that when utilizing state power the Church is not using any outside authority, but its own authority, granted to it by Christ. [17]

Hearing this, shouldn't the members of democratic parliaments quickly wake up?!
What else can that mean than: The state is fully in the clutches of the Church? And concerning the

authority allegedly granted by Christ – that can only be described as more lies. But who is the father of lies?

Deschner writes further about Augustine, Ratzinger's "friend":

And while already before flowed … streams of blood, in his time it continued with violent uprisings and turmoil: the stronger the state reacts, the louder Augustine applauds.
Here, the most celebrated church father shows himself in all his greatness: as the person pulling the levers and hypocrite; as a bishop who not only during his life brought about terrible things, but even more as the initiator of political Augustinianism: a prototype for all the Inquisitors dripping with blood throughout so many centuries, for their savagery, perfidy, bigotry, a pacesetter of horror and of the medieval relationship between church and state. Because Augustine's example allowed millions of people, even children and old people, the terminally-ill and crippled, to be shoved into the torture chambers by the secular office, into the darkness of the dungeons, the flames of the burning pyres – and to hypocritically request the state to spare their lives!

All future heretic-hunting, heretic-torturing, heretic-burning, henchmen and scoundrels, princes and monks, bishops and popes could and did base themselves on him – likewise the reformers.[18]

Jesus, the Christ – according to Doctor of the Church Augustine – also a "godless heretic"

In another place, it says about Augustine, Ratzinger's friend:

It wasn't hard for him to demonize the state, and to praise its bloody practices …

Anyone who thinks this way …, of course, also interprets the commandment "You shall not kill" accordingly. From the onset, it does not apply to all of nature and the animal world.

Neither does it forbid, polemicized Augustine against the Manichaeans, to "pull a flower," nor does it concern the "irrational animals," which are merely "subjected to us to kill or keep alive for our own uses": Subdue it … But to Augustine, man appears "even in the state of sin to indeed still be better than the animal," the creature of the "lowest rank." And he insulted vegetarianism as "a godless opinion of heretics".[19]

With one sentence, Augustine, Ratzinger's "friend," turns into "godless heretics" the apostles and early followers of the Nazarene, all of whom we cited here as being witnesses for vegetarianism.

According to church father Augustine, Peter and Paul are "godless heretics."

According to church father Augustine, the apostles Matthew, Mathias, John and James are "godless heretics," likewise Jerome, the translator of the Bible, nothing more than a "godless heretic," because he championed vegetarianism.

And ultimately, even Jesus, the Christ, according to Augustine, Ratzinger's friend, is nothing but a "godless heretic." Joseph Ratzinger calls such a word-twister of, very obviously, the worse kind, who was canonized by the Church, his "friend," and prays to him for support and help. What for?

Doesn't Jesus of Nazareth still ultimately hang on the cross in the Catholic Church because of such doctrines that disparage creation, even though He has risen long since? As a defeated trophy, as the "godless" vegetarian and "heretic," who condemned the slaughter of animals for sacrifice and eating meat as sins, and who exposed the priests and pointed out whom they in reality served and still do?

Augustine's thinking regarding the animals and nature was just as inhuman, brutal and high-handed as was his treatment of people. He claimed:

Must we therefore reckon it a breaking of this commandment, You shall not kill, to pull a flower? Are we thus insanely to countenance the foolish error of the Manicheans? We don't want to have anything to do with such insanity.[20]

But what Augustine described as the "foolish error" of the Manicheans is an aspect of the cosmic law of unity of man, nature and animals. And as the pinnacle of his displayed godless, and thus, satanic, thinking, he frankly admits: We don't want to have anything to do "with such insanity" – meaning the divine cosmic laws. Doesn't this statement in reality expose the primitive, base consciousness of the Catholic Doctor of the Church, Augustine, Ratzinger's "friend"?

Augustine theorized further, as usual, totally out of thin air:

Putting aside, then, these ravings, if, when we say, You shall not kill, we do not understand this of the plants, since they have no sensation, nor of the irrational animals that fly, swim, walk, or creep, since

> *they are dissociated from us by their want of reason, and are therefore by the just appointment of the Creator subjected to us to kill or keep alive for our own uses; if so, then it remains that we understand that commandment simply of man. The commandment is, "You shall not kill man;" therefore neither another nor yourself …*[21]

In another writing, Doctor of the Church Augustine, taught:

> *Cattle are not illuminated, because cattle have not rational minds capable of seeing wisdom. But man was made in the image of God, and has a rational mind, by which he can perceive wisdom.*[22]

It really takes a lot to turn out so much non-spirituality about the animals in the first place. To reveal so much spiritual ignorance only shows who Augustine was. Animals don't need wisdom "to see." They live in the wisdom of God. And is it supposed to be wisdom when one turns the teachings of Jesus of Nazareth into their opposite, as Augustine did? In any case, it's Catholic. It has nothing to do with wisdom, quite the opposite.

Perhaps that's one of the reasons why Augustine, Ratzinger's "friend," was canonized. If it wasn't so sad and wouldn't mean trillion-fold suffering for the animals, one could overlook it with compassion. But the terrible effects of these un-spiritual theories of Augustine are church doctrine until today – although even in the book by Josef Neuner and Heinrich Roos, "The Teaching of the Catholic Church," it says about Augustine:

Augustine himself confessed that the things he did not know were more than the things he did know.[23]

The cynical theories of the Doctor of the Church Thomas of Aquinas: Animals are destined for use

Another "friend" of Ratzinger, the Doctor of the Church Thomas of Aquinas, just like that, without any kind of spiritual background and spiritual knowledge, puts forth the following absurd theory:

"We declare that man alone has a subsistent soul," that is, a soul having life of itself; and that "the souls of brute animals perish along with their bodies." [24]

As we all know, anyone who declares something does not necessarily know it, which didn't keep the Church from cruelly torturing and having countless people killed by the millions, who believed, or even knew, something different, among them many vegetarians.

Even today every person must accept, that is, believe, this satanic delusion as the divine truth, if he doesn't want to be eternally damned. After all, this was believed or thought by a Doctor of the Church.

Furthermore, Thomas of Aquinas, Ratzinger's friend, claimed the following:

> *There is no sin in using a thing for the purpose for which it is. … Wherefore it is not unlawful if man use plants for the good of animals, and animals for the good of man … the life of animals and plants is preserved not for themselves but for man …* [25] *We cannot wish good things to an irrational creature, because it is not competent, properly speaking, to possess good …* [26]
>
> *A beast is by nature distinct from man, wherefore in the case of a wild beast there is no need for an authority to kill it; whereas, in the case of domestic animals, such authority is required, not for their sake, but on account of the owner's loss.* [27]

The following statement also comes from Thomas of Aquinas:

> *He that kills another's ox, sins, not through killing the ox, but through injuring another man in his property. Wherefore this is not a species of the sin of murder but of the sub of theft or robbery.*[28]

At this point, once more a quote from God's prophet Isaiah, to expose the contradiction, the falsification of the divine truth by the Church. God spoke through Isaiah:

> *He who slaughters an ox is like one who kills a man; he who sacrifices a lamb, like one who breaks a dog's neck; he who presents a grain offering, like one who offers pig's blood; he who makes a memorial offering of frankincense, like one who blesses an idol.* (Is. 66:3)

So, who's right? God's prophet Isaiah or the Doctor of the Church Thomas of Aquinas? Consequently, *either* the prophet of God Isaiah should be removed from the Bible – then it will be somewhat thinner – or Thomas of Aquinas should have his church honors disqualified, "de-sainted," so to speak, for being a false Doctor of the Church and false saint, a false teacher and heretic.

Concepts and opinions in church doctrine academically disproved long ago are still considered to be the measure of all things

Don't these contradictions demonstrate whom the Church serves? The Church obviously doesn't want to have anything to do with the prophets of God, and that, until today. But why?

The absurd concepts of such Doctors of the Church, whose theories have long since been disproved, for instance, regarding vegetarianism, are still considered to be the measure of all things from a Catholic point of view – and from these "Doctors of the Church," even former Pope Ratzinger requests support and help.

Research and science are also co-opted under compulsion and subliminally forced into obedience to the Church via the Catechism and the allegedly infallible church dogmas. We can read this in the collection of dogmas, "The Teaching of the Catholic Church as contained in Her Documents" by Neuner and Roos, under Margin Note No. 102:
> *Profane science should also concern itself with the noble task of Catholic exegesis.*

As if the knowledge of quantum physics should first have to receive the pope's permission that it exists!

Or let's take the statement following Margin Note No. 91:
> *But the Holy Scripture is the Word of God, and therefore, infallible. Scientific research can never leave this fact out of account ...there can be no contradiction between the words of the Holy Scripture and the findings of science ...*

And if natural science were to totally reduce the pipe dreams of the Doctors of the Church to ad absurdum – well, that cannot be, because the Doctors of the Church don't want this. And this, in the 21st century!

In Margin Note 95, the Vatican Church's official collection of dogmas continues:
> *Many attacks on Scripture are made in the field of the physical sciences. They are especially dangerous because of their attractive vividness.*

Jesus, the Christ, essentially says: The truth will make you free. – From what? Isn't it the churches and the external religions with their false teachings and sanctimonious priests, from which the truth liberates us, the phony and distorted rites, dogmas and ceremonies, which all stem from paganism?

Finally, Margin Note 96:

> *No real discord can exist between the theologian and the scientist provided each keeps within his own limits …*

In plain language to the scientists, this means: Keep your mouth shut and don't disturb our circles. Because it goes right on:

> *They should follow the warning of St. Augustine to beware of "affirming anything rashly, and the unknown as known. … Whatever they"* – that is, the physicists – *"propose in any books of theirs which is contrary to our scriptures, that is, to our Catholic faith, let us also show, if we are at all able, or at all events let us believe without any doubt that it is most false."*

Or as Christian Morgenstern expressed it in Palmström:

> *"… because," he utterly logically concludes, "nothing can be what may not be."*

Anyone who contradicts is eternally damned

And what if the independent natural sciences and the independent scholarship of history were to someday gain the upper hand over shaping public opinion, after all, and thus, all the Churches' terrible crimes were to come to light? Then the Church would still staunchly cling to the concept that all this atrocious truth – is simply lies! That's Catholic. – But if the lords of the Church were to really believe that the eternal Spirit of love, God, the Eternal, had appointed them, why then, do they have such a mortal fear of science?

But because that's not how it is, since God didn't call any priests or found any churches of stone – quite the contrary – a lot of scientific knowledge that doesn't fit into the calculation of the allegedly high clergy, or could decrease their immense claim to power, their avarice and self-interest, needs to be distorted in such a way that scientific knowledge, however groundbreaking and revolutionary it may be, is still "wrong" according to church doctrine. This is again the Catholic pattern. Let us not allow ourselves to be deceived – particularly where our nourishment, a vegetarian diet, is concerned. Many physicians and nutritionists know that a vegetarian diet is to be recommended for the human body purely for reasons of health. One can simply try it out.

That brings up another question: What do the catechisms and dogmas, the dogmatic declarations of the churches teach in case their so-called faithful contradict the church laws?

The answer: The sole alternative that Church law offers its sheep in case of disobedience to man-made church laws is eternal damnation! But no one has to believe such things! For God is love. He doesn't condemn any of His beloved children.

No earthly father would condemn his child eternally, and least of all God, the Eternal, who beheld and created us as His spiritual children. After all, with this, He would violate His own ironclad spiritual laws. The doctrine of eternal damnation is the work of man. It is one of the most malicious and most horrible mockeries of God by the priestmen; it is pure blasphemy.

Animal testing: Unimaginable cruelty blessed by the Church

A mockery of God, who respirates all Being, is also how man treats the animals in this world, which are man's fellow creatures, willed by God. They are treated so unspeakably cruelly, that their misery, that cries out to heaven, cannot be pointed out often enough and clearly enough. The animals are truly mercilessly delivered up to the criminal machination of the species man – and all this, with the blessing of the institutional, allegedly "Christian" churches, of the priests, bishops, cardinals and popes.

Let's go back to statements in the Catechism. It says there:

Medical and scientific experimentation on animals is a morally acceptable practice if it remains within reasonable limits and contributes to caring for or saving human lives. (Catholic Catechism, No. 2417)

What the Vatican under the pope's leadership actually understands under *"morally acceptable … within reasonable limits,"* one can conclude from the report by Radio Vatican on Dec. 10, 2011; we quote:

Pope Benedict appointed the neurophysiologist Prof. Wolf J. Singer as Consultant to the Pontifical Council for Culture. Already in 1992, he was appointed a lifelong member of the Pontifical Academy of Sciences.

What Prof. Wolf Singer, Director at the Max Planck Institute in Frankfurt for brain research, who was rewarded in this way for his loyalty to the church, really does to the animals, you can extensively read about in Internet. However, those reports are not for people with weak nerves!

Here are several excerpts with descriptions of experiments, of which Prof. Singer claims that, as a rule, the harm to the animals is less than the castration and sterilization of house pets.

Cats 3-5 weeks old were anesthetied and fixed in a so-called sterotactic frame, in order to ensure total immobility.

Further it says:

Through holes bored into the scull, Singer and his team put 27 tubes into the cerebral cortex. … after sewing the scalp together, the vivisectionists also scraped out one of the kitten's eyes. In case the animals survived, they were observed for weeks. For physiological recording sessions, the young cats were again anesthetized, totally paralyzed and artificially respirated.

After the end of each session, their blood was replaced with a fixer solution. Since good tissue specimens have to be taken from a living project, we can assume that for further examinations, the exchange of blood for formalin was done on the living animal. The cats' brains were removed, deep frozen, and then sliced, dyed and microscopically examined, in order to assess the extent of damage by the infusion tubes and in order to again find – if possible – the electrode pathways.

To "assess" or to "again find" something, God's creatures are bestially tortured here in the most brutal ways. Dr. Wolf Singer is infamous for his tests on cat and monkey brains. But someone who is against life, who is cruel to animals, very obviously gets promoted by the Vatican. That's the Catholic pattern.

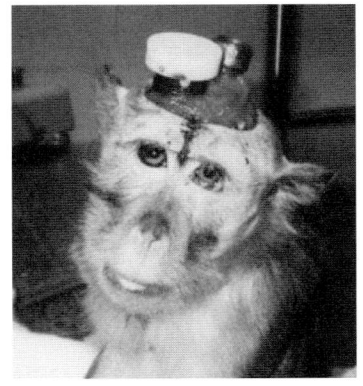

Nearly 3 million laboratory animals are "used" every year in German research laboratories alone. Of them, about 4000 are dogs and 800

cats. This makes about 11,500 lab animals that are murdered per workday or about 1400 animals per working hour.

It is not known how many of the vivisectionists nevertheless hypocritically call themselves Christian. It is only known that Paul said: "What a man sows, he will also reap."

Animal protectors and vegetarians are "heretics" – eternally damned by the Church

Let us realize that all this sadistic torturing is blessed by the churches. On the other hand, when someone, for example, as an advocate for animals, claims that animals have a soul and that this research is deviant and perverse, then this is considered the same as a violation of church law. In the eyes of the Church, anyone who thinks and speaks this way is a heretic. If a disobedient Catholic disregards only one of the dogmas, rites and cults that are directed against life, only one of the sometimes abstruse and brutal doctrinal statements of men, of whom, according to present-day law, many with great certainty would have to be handed over to the law, then, inevitably, he is threatened with eternal damnation. But aside from this, all people who are not Catholic are threatened with this; presently this is at least 5.5 billion people. And so, all Moslems, all Jews, all atheists, all Buddhists, all Hindus, etc., for according to Catholic doctrine, there is no salvation outside the Church.

Based on the democratic constitution in Germany, the eradication of heretics – and animal welfare as well as vegetarianism were always considered a main indication of heresy – is presently postponed to an undetermined time. But until today, every Catholic is compelled to acknowledge all these doctrines of eradication without exception. Otherwise, this means, even for the best Catholics – away, and into eternal damnation with you!

Let us realize that the Catholic Church teaches that all vegetarians on Earth are still godless heretics and eternally damned, because the Doctor of the Church Augustine, the "saint," wanted it this way! Augustine, Ratzinger's special friend, whom he asks for support and help!

Let us realize that the Catholic Church teaches that all vegetarians on Earth are still godless heretics and eternally damned, because at the First Synod of Braga, Pope John III (561-574) declared vegetarians to be excommunicated:

If anyone considers the foods of the flesh unclean, which God has given for the use of men ... but ... so abstains from these ... let him be anathema.[29]

And until today, this threat of excommunication hasn't been rescinded. On the contrary, it can be found in the official and extensive collection of dogmas by Heinrich Denzinger and Adolf Schönmetzer.

We need to realize that in the Middle Ages a declaration of excommunication amounted to a death sentence, because it constituted "being declared fair game." Anyone could even kill an excommunicated person without being punished. As a person excluded from society he automatically lost all rights. – By the way, how do the animal friends and vegetarians in the churches feel about this, or have all of them already left the Church?

**"She [the Church] must therefore
with painstaking care, remove and eradicate
anything that is contrary to faith ..."**

In the "Teaching of the Catholic Church as Contained in Her Documents", 1965, by Neuner and Roos, we read under Margin Note No. 352:
She [meaning the Church] *must therefore with painstaking care remove and eradicate anything that is contrary to faith…*

This means, that if you, dear reader, believe that your animal has a soul, or that animals, in general, have a soul, and that animals should be given love, then, according to current church law, you should be eradicated. – Are you aware of this?
According to Webster's dictionary, eradicate means: to do away with completely!
That is the binding and current doctrine of the Catholic Church!

The Church had all true followers of Jesus of Nazareth defamed, persecuted, murdered or eradicated – all those who wanted something different – namely as Jesus of Nazareth taught us. That is the institutional church mindset, its ethics and morals. That is its highly praised Catholic tradition.

But the former Catholic Martin Luther was also deeply influenced by this, as the cruel, bloodthirsty slaughter and execution of countless peasants, "witches" and so-called heretics prove, all of which happened at his instigation.

**Upright followers of Christ,
yes, entire Christian communities of faith,
were bloodily persecuted by the Church**

Already during the first centuries after Christ, the followers of the Nazarene, who were exclusively vegetarians – otherwise they would not have been admitted into the first communities at all – were bloodily persecuted and brutally eradicated. They were stigmatized as heretics, and in cruel blood-baths, tortured, burned, enslaved, massacred and eradicated by the tens of thousands.
It was Christian communities of faith, such as the Manicheans, Bogumils and Paulicians, Waldensians, Cathars and Hussites, which were simply murdered as heretics at the instigation of the Church. It was people like Marcion, Montana, Maximilla, Priscilla, Mani, Origen, Jan Hus, Giordano Bruno, Savonarola and many more upright followers of Christ, all

people, who were determined to have Jesus of Nazareth resurrect in themselves, to follow Him in the deed and in all freedom, and who were resolved to let their spiritual knowledge about the life, which God is, become reality in everyday life.

But then, again and again, the merciless, relentless religious competition came, the deadly pact between state and church, which made life on Earth already hell for the people, with fire and sword and with the doctrine of eternal damnation invented by the priests instead of the teaching of reincarnation.
Over and over again, right into the most recent past, an aggressive caste of priests incited individual nations against minorities and against other nations. And the high clergy cried out: "God wants this! God wants this! God with us!"
With fire and sword, with murder and manslaughter, through torture and enslavement, for centuries, they beat, drummed and hammered into the people the exact opposite of what Jesus of Nazareth taught. They poured their truly demonic, animal-cannibalistic doctrine into the wounded and mangled bodies and into the sore souls of the oppressed nations. And again and again, an aggressive high clergy ranted: God wants this! Serve authority! Anyone who does

not obey the Church and the state will not only land in the dungeon or on the pyre or on the gallows, but also in eternal damnation. Gods wants this! God with us!

And in huge bloody massacres, culminating in world wars, they preached the same thing all over again and on all sides of the fronts: "God wants this! God wants this!" And while they did this, the mountains of corpses were piling up higher and higher on the battlefields, and the mangled nations were depopulated, until hardly anyone was left alive to put a stop to the satanic doings. All the more easily, could the properties of the victims then be snared to increase the wealth of the Church, and above all, the personal wealth of its officials. That is church history. That is the true tradition of the churches, cultivated over centuries. And the so-called "Saint" Paul says: "What a man sows, he will also reap."

As stated, the lords of the Church brought to the people that had been bled dry and intimidated the following:
- Eternal damnation –
  instead of the truth, namely the teaching of reincarnation and the law of cause and effect.

- The pagan cult of priests, with blood offerings and eating meat –
  instead of a lawful vegetarian diet.
- The alleged honors of military service, because they wanted to wage war and they needed the human slaughter animal for this –
  instead of pacifism, the love of enemy of Jesus of Nazareth.

Thus, the Catholic Church became big and bigger, richer and richer, immeasurably rich, as rich, as one imagines the whore of Babylon to be. But hardly anyone thinks anything of this or asks whether the devil now resides in the Church.

Emperor Constantine turned Christianity into a state religion – the fight against the peace-loving, vegetarian followers of Jesus of Nazareth became even more brutal

Roman Emperor Constantine played a decisive role in turning the people away from the teaching of love for God and neighbor, from the principles of equality, freedom, unity, brotherliness and justice, which Jesus of Nazareth taught.

When in 324 Christianity was co-opted by Emperor Constantine and, for tactical political reasons, was turned into a state religion, the new alliance of church and state fought for its old pagan sinecures, against the followers of Jesus of Nazareth, of whom many were vegetarians – and they fought against these so-called heretics with even greater brutality.

These truly were campaigns of pure annihilation, the worst massacres against peaceful people, whose greatest "offence" consisted of doing and trying to fulfill what Jesus of Nazareth had taught, which also included not eating meat. They were persecuted and eradicated – also because they did not bow to the will of the pagan priests, who now called themselves "Christian," but instead, listened to the prophetic word of the Christ of God, the inner word, which was given to some of them, in order to lead the communities according to His will.

For having raised the then already secularized external Christianity to the state religion, which now had nothing, absolutely nothing more at all, to do with what Jesus of Nazareth taught, Emperor Constantine was later canonized – totally according to the popular saying: Birds of a feather flock together.

But Emperor Constantine was in no way second to any of his predecessors in terms of megalomania, imperiousness and cruelty. He waged many wars. Followers of Jesus of Nazareth who wanted to remain faithful to their pacifist ideals were now forced, under threat of torture, to go to war for the Emperor. It is said that when someone did not want to eat meat, Emperor Constantine had molten lead poured down their throat.

Due to the persecution and eradication of the followers of Jesus of Nazareth, Early Christianity was nearly wiped out. Christians were now officially forced to perform military service, to eat animals and to drink alcohol. Only these so-called "Christians" were spared persecution.

In the "Kriminalgeschichte des Christentums" by K.H. Deschner, we read what Percy Bysshe Shelley wrote about Constantine:

> ...this monster Constantine ... This cold-blooded and hypocritical brute slit his son's throat, strangled his wife, murdered his father-in-law and his brother-in-law and maintained at his court a clique of bloodthirsty and bigoted Christian priests, of whom one single one would have been enough to stir up one half of mankind to slaughter the other half.[30]

Heretics were condemned to death by the Church. The distinguishing characteristic of a heretic: He is vegetarian

The persecution of vegetarian Christians continued in the Middle Ages. They were denigrated as heretics and sectarians, defamed, persecuted and murdered.

The philosophical foundation for persecution during the Middle Ages was laid by Doctor of the Church, Thomas of Aquinas. In his opinion, animals do not have immortal souls and, in comparison to men, women are merely inferior beings, a "misbegotten" man. Thomas literally writes:
> *As regards the individual nature, woman is defective and misbegotten, for the active force in the male seed tends to the production of a perfect likeness in the masculine sex; while the production of woman comes from defect in the active force or from some material indisposition* ...[31]

But Thomas of Aquinas, too, is former Pope Ratzinger's "friend." He prays to this so-called saint. The question is, for what?
Are the many women still within the Church even aware of these statements by Thomas of Aquinas –

the allegedly holy "Doctor of the Church" – that denigrate women in the worst way? It's hardly likely. Let's take a further look into the gruesome times of the Middle Ages. The philosopher Count von Hoensbroech writes, for instance:

As a result of a Bishops' Conference in Goslar in the year 1051, several were condemned to death as heretics, because they had refused to kill chickens, since this corresponded to the ideology of the Cathars not to kill animals.[32]

In the 13th century, two women in southern France were handed over as "heretics" and executed, because they refused to kill a chicken.[33]

In the book by K.H. Deschner "Opus Diaboli," it says about this:

We know Catholics who in the 13th century declared their orthodoxy with the oath: I am not a heretic, because I have a wife and sleep with her; I have children and eat meat, I lie, curse and am a faithful Christian, so help me God![34]

Well now, that's truly an unspoilt Catholic creed! Here you know exactly where you stand! Wouldn't that be something to hang up in the classrooms next to the crucifix? Or in courtrooms and other public buildings, always next to the crucifix (a common practice in Bavaria, Germany)? Or perhaps it would even be something for the German Parliament?

And so, countless people were persecuted merely because they took the teachings of Jesus of Nazareth seriously; they were vegetarians and thus, also respected the life in animals and nature. So we can say that because they strove for a life of higher ethics and morals and higher values than did the Catholic leadership and its murderous vassals, they were bestially tortured and murdered.

Millionfold and billionfold:
Horror under the guise of "Christian"

For once, let us become aware of the full range of clerical monstrosities: Murder, torture, mutilate, burn, subjugate, rape, enslave and practice all sadistic atrocities, which only psychically sick brains can think up – and all this, unceasingly.
There were countless victims, for centuries. The atrocities were practiced millionfold and billionfold, "come hell or high water."

Wars were instigated and they waged war themselves. There were wars of extermination against the born life, Christians against heathens and Jews, Christians against Moslems and Indians, then later Christians against Christians, and all together, against the life of the animals, which is from God, for there is no life outside of God. The historic facts confirm the deeds, or better said, misdeeds, of the Church. Apparently, this is their so vaunted "tradition," which particularly the politicians with the "C" for Christian in their party names like to refer to! The next time you hear the words and hymns of praise about the allegedly oh-so-splendid Catholic tradition, then you know for sure what it's really all about.

Until today, the genuine love for animals and nature, the respect for life – that is, for *all* life – and the recognition that in all things and everyone is God, the Creator, and the freedom in His Spirit, because He, God, the Eternal, is the free Spirit – this was and is "the work of the devil" for the churches and their servile vassals in politics.

Apparently, the following applies: Free, upright people, who think as Jesus of Nazareth lived as an example and taught, should be ostracized and are not wanted in the country, above all, when they also work for the rehabilitation of Jesus, the Christ, and openly address the deception, the colossal fraudulent labeling of the churches.

Such people are not wanted – and they are, as ever, persecuted even today by the churches, which appoint their own so-called "sect commissioners," to incite the people against the "heretics" of our days. But why are there actually the so-called sect commissioners of the institutional churches in Germany, yes, even those of the state that is servile to the church, when freedom of religion is anchored in the Constitution? It would also be worthwhile to think about this. The judiciary is responsible for legal offences; that should be sufficient in a democratic state where the law expressly requires the separation of church and state. Here, too, Germany is quite unique. Anyone who does not bow to the dogmas, rites, ceremonies, cults, which are confining and hostile to life, and to the ecclesiastically authoritative mentality derived only from itself, is, until today, more or less an enemy of meat-eating society, and thus, according to Augustine, a "godless heretic"! In the eyes of this society, the animal with a soul is merely a piece of livestock, which is meant to be killed and eaten, and it must bring a profit, for all its worth. This is their true ethics, the Catholic ethics, the Lutheran-Protestant ethics, which, however, is increasingly leading mankind into the abyss.

Until just a few years ago, vegetarians were persecuted and demonized by "sect commissioners," because their diet was supposedly dangerous to health, and the press greedily took up these defamations. That, too, is Germany!

Do not eat the suffering of the animals!

Dear readers, inform yourselves and then decide how you want to live in relation to the animals. The concern of this book is that more and more people recognize how bestially animals are treated, and that they begin to follow a vegetarian diet. Above all in Internet, there are many websites that can help you to get out of the cycle of the un-good, the share of the blame for the suffering of the animals. If you would like to, begin to slowly change your eating habits. For example, prepare a vegetarian meal on several days in the week. Gradually change your diet. With some people it goes faster, others need somewhat more time. No matter. It will get better from day to day. You will see that it will become a gain in life for you, not only because vegetarian meals are healthier – your soul will also profit from this.

> Therefore: *Eat no meat!*
> *Do not eat the suffering of the animals!*
> Eating meat is truly against the law of life, which is God.

The origin of the millionfold suffering of the animals: Church law

The disregard for all life, especially the bestial animal massacres in the slaughterhouses of this world, the whole satanic way of treating the animals and nature ultimately goes back to church law, to the dogmas and doctrines of the churches, which justify the destruction of all forms of life, and, considered carefully, even demonize Jesus, the Christ, and His apostles, as "godless heretics," because they were vegetarian!
According to church law, all animal and plant life on the Earth, in the oceans, in the air is free to be murdered, because it is here only for human consumption. – This is the churches' satanic exploitative interpretation of the millionfold-abused statement: Subdue the Earth!

Let us ask ourselves: How could people degenerate so far ethically and morally; how could they sink so low, even though Jesus of Nazareth brought people the teaching of peace and unity between humans, nature and animals, the teachings of the Sermon on the Mount? How can it be that all the despicable crimes committed by people on animals and nature

are silently tolerated by the majority of people, yes, often literally viewed as totally normal, and that within a few decades, this behavior will make the dwelling planet Earth largely uninhabitable?
How could things go so far? Who wants this?
Where does such a comprehensive manipulation, yes, brainwashing, come from?

The hunt:
Torture and death blessed by priests

To many people, it still appears totally normal that, for example, to a dramatic extent, more and more habitats are taken away from the animals living in the wild, and that from concealed ambushes, high-caliber weapons and projectiles with the most perverse effect are used to shoot the life from their bodies, or the limbs from their bodies – and that, with priestly blessing? Is that still normal? Is that Christian?

No – it is Catholic or Protestant-Lutheran – no more. Regarding this, a statement from the book "Totentanz der Tiere" by Harald Voss und Dr. Gunter Bleibohm:

Events to bless the animals and individual actions at church conferences serve solely as alibi functions, but they do not remedy the fundamental lack of the mainstream churches in being totally disinterested in the suffering of the animals. In this case, opportunistic behavior is not merely an evil; here, it is a crime against the animals![35]

Lured, hunted, chased, shot and wounded, caught in traps and brought down with further bestialities, the noble creatures of God die in the cruelest ways through the brutality of man with no conscience – and often only after many suffering-filled hours or days. Only 25-30% of hunted animals are killed by a so-called heart shot.

Many of the "leaded," that is, grazed, animals – that is, shot and wounded – are not found during the search for them, if this is even carried out, at all. The whole thing is called "the hunt" and the bagged "line of animals laid out on display" is often blessed by so-called "Christian," but, in actuality, merely Catholic or Protestant-Lutheran, priests. Let's ask ourselves: Did Jesus of Nazareth teach anything like this? Who wants this? Who condones it? Who blesses this in whose name?

Factory farming:
Suffering and misery blessed by the Church

It's even worse for the so-called "livestock animals" that have virtually no habitats at all any more and are conceded only a short life of vegetation, often under bestial and sadistic conditions, by those in the western world called "Christians," before they – the cows, pigs, sheep, turkeys, chickens and many other animals – are murdered in the cruelest way, not seldom, still alive and writhing on the conveyor belt because of insufficient anesthetization. Afterward, they are devoured in the animal-cannibal manner. And all this in numbers that one can't even grasp anymore.

Jonathan Safran Foer writes in his book "Eating Animals":
Globally, roughly 450 billion land animals are now factory farmed every year.[36]

Can we at all imagine what it means to kill about 450 billion animals as slaughter animals – tendency rising?
Can we imagine 450 billion – billion! – animal carcasses? How large is this sea of blood?

During the brevity of this portrayal, it is not possible to point out all the atrocities and perversities that are committed on animals. But as an example of the tremendous suffering of the animals, we will cite a few facts. Did you know that in Europe alone, about 400 million rabbits are raised annually for the fur and meat industry? Do you have any idea of how endlessly gruesome such a life in a cage is? And many other animal species that are trapped or raised for the fur industry experience hell on Earth. Inform yourself. There is enough information on various websites in Internet, above all, about the fur industry and factory farming.

The following numbers on factory farming are based on a study published in 2008 by the German Federal Bureau of Statistics:
Approximately 98% of the animals in Germany kept for consumption stemmed from factory farms: with cattle it's 95.7%, with pigs 99.3%, and with poultry 97.9%.

At the end of the German edition of the book "Eating Animals" by Jonathan Foer, there is a summary of the situation in Germany, excerpts of which are given here. According to this, approximately 56.5 million pigs, 3.8 million cows, calves and young cattle, 1.05 million sheep and lambs, about 28,000 goats, 9,400 horses are slaughtered annually.

Per year, hatch as "chicks to be fattened for slaughter": 585 million broiler chicks, 25.5 million ducklings, 1.03 million goslings, 44.8 million baby turkeys and guinea fowl. In addition, about 40 million so-called "female laying chicks," hatch that are raised for egg production.

Naturally, for every female chick, a male chick also hatches, which can't be used for egg production and is killed. Consequently, about 40 million male chicks are gassed or shredded alive every year.

Germany's annual per capita consumption of meat is 83.3 kilograms. Added to this, are 16 kilos of fish per capita per year.

Mankind is waging a merciless war against the animals and nature, on land, water and in the air! In the truest sense of the word, it is a total war – a cruel war of extermination against the life, everywhere, which eclipses anything imaginable.

However: All animals have the same breath as we humans do. Animals love freedom beyond all measure. Inform yourself about so-called livestock farming, and especially about factory farming. Above all, in Internet, there are enough websites to give you a comprehensive picture.

In the face of this immeasurable suffering, once more the appeal:
Eat no meat! Do not eat the suffering of the animals!

The oceans are being fished empty

There are no exact numbers for the worldwide consumption of fish. However, it has indeed been determined that by the year 2050 the oceans will be fished empty to such an extent that there will be hardly anymore life in them worth mentioning.

Several publications state that over 120 million tons of fish are taken annually from the oceans. A third of them are the so-called bycatch, which is either thrown overboard or processed into fish meal. Bycatch could be whales, sharks, dolphins, marine birds, turtles, in short, anything at all!

Jonathan Safran Foer writes further:
Our situation is so extreme that research scientists at the Fisheries Centre of the University of British Columbia argue that "our interactions with fisheries resources (also known as fish) have come to resemble ... wars of extinction."[37]
Technologies of war have literally and systematically been applied to fishing. Radar, echo sounders, navy-developed electronic navigation systems, satellite-based GPS ... Satellite-generated images of ocean temperatures are used to identify fish schools.

> *Once the picture of industrial fishing is filled in – the 1.4 billion hooks that are deployed annually on long lines (on each of which is a chunk of fish, squid or dolphin flesh used as bait); the 1200 nets, each 30 miles (50 km) in length, used by only one fleet to catch only one species; the ability of one single vessel to haul in 50 tons of sea animals in a few minutes – it becomes easier to think of contemporary fishers as factory farmers rather than fishermen.*[38]

Can you imagine what 60,000 kilometers of nets mean? That's 1.5 times the Earth's circumference. And that, for only one fleet that usually catches only one species.

Fish are also sentient beings!

In another place in the book "Eating Animals" by Jonathan Safran Foer, we can learn the following about fish: Fish also have a spine and pain receptors; they produce endorphins to relieve pain. Fish show all of the familiar pain responses.

> *Fish build complex nests, form monogamous relationships, hunt cooperatively with other species, and use tools. They recognize each other as individuals (and keep track of who is to be trusted and who not.) They*

make decisions individually, and monitor social prestige and vie for better positions… They have significant long-term memories, are skilled in passing knowledge to one another through social networks, and can also pass on information generationally. They even have what scientific literature calls "long-standing 'cultural traditions' for particular pathways to feeding, schooling, resting or mating sites." ³⁹

We, mankind, respect the habitat of the ocean just as little as everything else. We leave behind several huge whirlpools of plastic trash in the oceans, with a diameter of hundreds of kilometers, hundreds of meters high, drifting at a depth of up to a few hundred meters. Countless marine dwellers also die from this, because they think the plastic trash is food. – All totally normal, right?!

Animal massacre: Condoned by high-ranking church functionaries

All this and even much more, all the cruelty and brutality toward animals, the blood shedding and slaughtering at an unimaginable magnitude, takes place in the western world under the ethical-moral leadership of the institutional churches, Catholics under the leadership of a pope, who, for his part, rejoices over deer carcasses and castrated roosters, called capons, and this, as the alleged vicar of Christ! – All totally normal, right? That is the call: "Subdue the Earth!" as the priests want to understand it – but God did not want this!

Aside from the pope, there are other high-ranking "role models" for shedding blood and slaughtering: In 2011 on the occasion of an artisan celebration at the construction site in the Hildesheim cathedral, that is, in the middle of the cathedral (!) – "a suckling pig swam in its broth" as the bishopric proudly reported. Also normal, right?

And the Archbishop of Munich and Freising, Reinhard Marx, stated that in his opinion, butchering is a part of Christianity, and he can still remember well "how butchering was done at home: We were always allowed to stir the pail full of blood!"[40]

The Church has passed off this animal killing cult to the people as "Christian" for long enough – but the cult of blood and slaughter belongs to Catholicism, not to Christianity!

For Jesus, the Christ, says:

> *Verily, I say to you, the one who derives benefit from the injustice that is inflicted on a creature of God cannot be righteous. Just as little can those whose hands are stained with blood or whose mouths are defiled with flesh deal with holy matters or teach the mysteries of heaven.* (The Gospel of the Holy Twelve, Chap. 38:2)

The behavior of ecclesiastical leading figures clearly demonstrates what dark forces the church quite obviously serves until today. Church history is truly written in unimaginably large quantities of blood – it's the blood of countless innocent people and of many trillions of innocent animals. Trillions!

Note well: The war of extermination against the animals and nature primarily takes place in a society that hypocritically calls itself "Christian" in the western world and for whom the mass murder of animals, the massacre of animals for the "Christian" holidays such as Easter and Christmas, are a matter of course.

All this is done with the blessing of the externalized churches. And for the people, the threat of "eternal damnation" is still in force, in case there are some lemmings who would veer away from the flock because they might begin to use their heart and their mind – from the Church's point of view, a sacrilege anyway – in order to renounce the customary, bloody, barbaric paganism that calls itself "Christian." And perhaps to begin to gradually expand their own consciousness and to fulfill step by step what Jesus of Nazareth taught us in His Sermon on the

Mount and thus, not what the churches teach, above all regarding the treatment of nature and animals.

Easter and Christmas: Animal massacres of enormous dimensions and rivers of blood as the high point of the institutional "Christian" church calendar year shape the western sham-Christian society, year in and year out. That it is thereby under the fatally wrong view of being somewhat civilized, but for the most part has a heart of stone and is far from the recognition of what ethics, morals and civilization mean, bears witness to the ethical and moral all-time-low of this society. This applies particularly and especially to the churches that call themselves Christian, which have had the people under their thumb for 2000 years – and not lastly, to the political parties that call themselves Christian. Otherwise, this world would very probably not despise life as much as it does.

The church solemnities of Easter and Christmas in institutional "Christianity" are secretly preceded by a truly bestial slaughter feast. Basically, the so-called Christians celebrate a pagan blood feast without equal and, historically confirmable, an image of paganism and barbarity, of the most primitive blood sacrifice traditions. which are today found only in a few Stone Age aboriginal peoples in the last jungles of this Earth!

Where animals and nature are concerned, many – let it be emphasized: not all – of the ostensibly Christian people of the present generation act worse than people who have never in their lives heard anything about higher ethical and moral values. In the western world, this takes place under the ethical-moral leadership of the institutional Catholic and Protestant Churches, which have accepted none of the spiritual principles that the Christ of God taught us, as binding guidelines for daily life, and apparently have absolutely no concept of the creation of God, who is the life in all things and in all.

Therefore, the appeal:
Eat no meat! Do not eat the suffering of the animals!

History shows that animals were formerly sacrificed directly in the temple precincts. This is why Jesus of Nazareth took the whip to drive the animal merchants out of the temple.

In what has been passed down, we hear about the cleansing of the temple:

And he entered the temple and began to drive out those who sold and those who bought in the temple, and he overturned the tables of the money-changers and the seats of those who sold pigeons. ... And he was teaching them and saying to them: "Is it not written: 'My house shall be called a house of prayer for all the nations'? But you have made it a den of robbers." (Mark 11:14-17)

So He did not speak of a temple for Catholics. He spoke of a temple for all nations. He who has ears to hear, let him hear!

Today the mass slaughters no longer take place in a temple-den-of-robbers, no longer in the temple courtyard, but in the anonymity of industrial areas, in a den for slaughter, a slaughterhouse, which is hell for the animals.

Then later, the sacrificial meal is prepared in a kitchen and demolished in the dining room of the apartment or house, perhaps also in the anonymity of a sausage stand or the like, culminating in the dining temples of many a star chef, who even practice their gruesome animal cannibalism on TV shows and try to implant it in the imitators, as if they had never heard of the correlations between factory farming and the climate collapse, to say nothing of ethics. Approximately 290 million tons of meat were "produced" in the year 2011.

We've already heard about how many animals that approximately is. Hundreds of billions of sentient living beings, most of them animal children, which – as researched by scientists – do have a consciousness, are murdered in bestial ways, so that they can be eaten in the animal-cannibal fashion.

290 million tons of meat in one year. By the year 2050, it's predicted to be 460 million tons of meat annually.

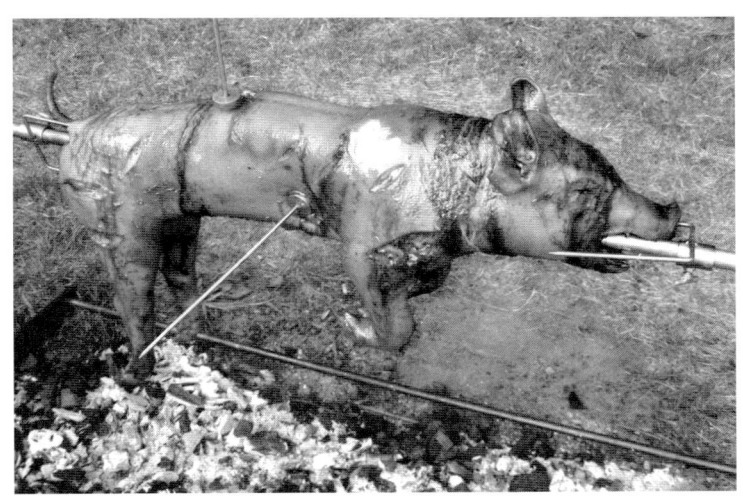

Physics says: No energy is lost.
Paul says: What a man sows, he will also reap.
Jesus, the Christ, says:

Verily, I say to you, I Am come into the world in order to put an end to all blood offerings and to the eating of the flesh of animals and birds that are slain by men. (Gospel of the Holy Twelve, Chap. 74:9)

Therefore, once more the request:
Eat no meat! Do not eat the suffering of the animals!

Did Jesus of Nazareth eat meat and fish?

Dear reader, again and again people point out that it is reported of Jesus of Nazareth that He multiplied bread, fruit and fish – and yes, that He allegedly also ate meat. In the great work of revelation "This Is My Word, Alpha and Omega,"[41] Christ gives the following explanation on pages 379-382 as follows:

On that day, dead fish were also offered to Me in order to be multiplied. As I took this dead substance into My hands, I explained to the people that the power-potential of the Father, the high power of life, was gone from it for the most part and that I would not create live fish so that they be killed again. ... "I will not give you living fish from the Spirit of the Father; but – from the energy of the Earth – I will create for you fish that are dead, that is, poor in vibration. They will never bear life and cannot be killed. I will show you how living things – bread and fruits – taste, and in comparison with them, the taste of the dead food."

Further Christ revealed:

... every abrupt break with old habits is fanaticism. In the one who lets go of his old habits from one minute to the next, an abrupt break takes place and not a transformation. In this abrupt break, there lies the seed for a renewed outbreak of the old suppressed habits
...
Thus, old habits should not be abruptly stopped, but it should be a gradual letting go that leads to a transformation in which the person turns to higher goals and values. This is a spiritual departure to new shores
...
And so, with the multiplication of the fishes, I showed that man should transform and not castigate himself. Every transformation is accomplished in a law-abiding way; it is the complete change from a lower to a higher life. Thus, transformation is the change from what is

human to what is spiritual. In this lies the gradual letting go of humanness and at the same time the awakening of spiritual divineness.

Often objections are made like the following: "But Jesus also ate meat…" Regarding this, we continue reading in the Christ-Revelation "This Is My Word" – Christ says:

Neither the apostles nor the disciples gave the order to slaughter a lamb. But as a gift of love, parts of a prepared lamb were offered to Me as well as to the apostles and disciples. With this, our neighbors wanted to make a gift for us, for they did not know better. I blessed the gift and began to partake of the meat. My apostles and disciples did the same. Afterwards, they asked Me in the following sense: We should refrain from consuming meat. This is what You have commanded of us. Now You, Yourself, have consumed meat.

I instructed My own that man should not willfully kill an animal nor should he consume the meat of animals which were killed for the consumption of their meat. However, when people who are still unknowing have prepared meat as nourishment and make of it a gift to the guest, offering it with the meal, then the guest should not reject the gift. For there is a difference whether a person consumes meat because he craves for meat or as a token of gratitude to the host for his effort.

However, when it is possible for him and outer circumstances and time permit, the knowing person should give general indications to the host, but should not want to set him right. When the time is ripe, the host, too, will understand these general indications.

In this world, understanding and tolerance, too, are aspects of selfless love. Leave to each person his free will whether or not he wants to understand and accept your general indications. If you think, speak and act selflessly at all times, you abide in love and love will bless you. What is then offered to you as a gift of love is blessed. (pp. 804-805)

Let us realize once more that following the example of Jesus of Nazareth, the first Christians were pacifists, conscientious objectors – and animal protectors. They kept the commandment of God "You shall not kill" and refused to eat the flesh of their fellow creatures.

However, Jesus' teaching of peace and love for all creatures was falsified and replaced with dogmas, rites and the priesthood of an external cult religion, which was forced on the people, often even with the use of threats and brutal violence. Vegetarians were then called "godless heretics" – they were persecuted and many were mercilessly eradicated.

The Doctor of the Church, Thomas of Aquinas, established for his church that animals do not have an immortal soul. The Doctor of the Church, Augustine, even talks about *"the irrational animal world," which merely is "subjected to us to kill or keep alive for our own uses."*[42]

And with the contribution of Joseph Ratzinger, the Church teaches today in the Catholic Catechism:

Hence it is legitimate to use animals for food and clothing. ... Medical and scientific experimentation on animals is a morally acceptable practice if it remains within reasonable limits ... (No. 2417)

The result of this doctrine hostile to life is the unimaginable cruelty toward the animal world and a bloodbath of monstrous extent: the brutal slaughter of billions of animals every year, because man traditionally eats meat.

Animals suffer under bestial pain and torment, inflicted upon them by man. Just think of the animals in the animal experimental laboratories; think of the animals in the wild that fall victim to senseless hunting. Fish in nets and on hooks have to suffocate in agony when they are jerked out of the water.

Huge whales are often cut up while still alive. Dogs are eaten in 44 countries of this world and often they are skinned alive, because then they allegedly taste better. Baby seals, that can hardly crawl over the ice yet, are beaten to death or shot before the eyes of their screaming mothers, by coarse men, who call themselves seal hunters, only so that they can skin them for their pelts, and at that, often while still alive, as well.

The unimaginable horror in the barns and slaughterhouses

Until now, only a few examples of the cruelties that man practices on his fellow creatures were described. When it's about man getting a piece of meat on his plate, the extent of the bloodshed is so enormous that we can hardly imagine it – as stated: Every year billions (!) of so-called farm animals vegetate away in the barns of factory farming, to be slaughtered in the end. But unimaginable and unknown to most people, are the cruelties that the animals are helplessly exposed to in the slaughterhouse. For this reason, we want to look more closely at the meat production industry and listen, particularly with the question: How is meat "produced"? Who really knows what it looks like in the slaughterhouses of this world? Who really knows what is done there to the animals and how it is for the people?

Mankind, with its truly satanic excesses, degrades the life of animals everywhere into an insentient commodity. Man either does not want to see the result of this – or he is indifferent to it, since gruesome executions and dismemberment of living animals are the order of the day.

In a survey of beef plants by Temple Grandin, a slaughterhouse inspector:

... fully 25 percent of the slaughterhouses had abuses so severe that they automatically failed her audit.[43]

Inform yourself, take a close look! There are enough websites in Internet that provide information about this horror.

There is a lot of literature and clarification, particularly on factory farming and the mass murder of animals, so that people who still have at least a remnant of awareness for ethical and moral values and a bit of good will can seriously concern themselves with the path to vegetarianism as a way out of all the horror.

But apparently, the centuries-long influence and threats against people by way of church law – above all, the abominable teaching of an alleged eternal damnation, which Jesus never taught – still sit deep in people's subconscious as a scarcely conquerable fear, so that not all people with a clear mind realize the following:

The monstrous brutality with which animals and nature are exploited and maltreated today has its roots in the archaic priest cults and dogmatic teachings of the institutional churches. They abuse the name "Christian" for their pagan cults and traditions, including the justification of the monumental worldwide animal cannibalism – namely, and above all, through the statements of contempt of nature, made by the Doctors of the Church Augustine and Thomas of Aquinas, who, according to his own statement, are "friends" of former Pope Joseph Ratzinger, and through the Roman emperor and butcher Constantine.

Jonathan Safran Foer writes in his book "Eating Animals":
… the livestock sector contributes 40% more to global warming than the entire transport sector worldwide; it is cause no. 1 for the climate change.[44]

Dr. Stanley Curtis … a livestock researcher … evaluated the cognitive abilities of pigs:
… They not only learned video games, but did so as fast as chimpanzees, demonstrating a surprising capacity for abstract representation.[45]

The bottom line in Jonathan Foer's book is that meat-eaters have only one choice, between cruelty and ecological destruction on the one hand, and the decision not to eat animals on the other hand.

> *Even in abattoirs where most cattle die quickly, it's hard to imagine that any day passes in which numerous animals (tens, hundreds?) don't meet an end of the most horrifying kind…*
> *A steel bolt shoots into the cow's skull … Sometimes the bolt only dazes the animal, which either remains conscious or later wakes up as it is being "processed."*[46]

> *Animals are bled, skinned, and dismembered while conscious. It happens all the time, and industry and government know it. Several plants cited for bleeding or skinning or dismembering live animals have defended their actions as common in the industry …*

We have to repeat that: They *"defend their actions as common in the industry …"!*

It says further:
> *When Temple Grandin conducted an industrywide audit in 1996, her studies revealed that the vast majority of cattle slaughterhouses were unable to regularly render cattle unconscious with a single blow.*[47]

The slaughterhouse inspector,
> *Temple Grandin has argued that ordinary people can become sadistic from the dehumanizing work of constant slaughter.*[48]

In Jonathan Foer's book "Eating Animals," we find the following report by a worker:

> *I've seen thousands and thousands of cows go through the slaughter process alive. … The cows can get seven minutes down the line and still be alive. I've been in the side puller where they're still alive. All the hide is stripped off from the neck down there.*[49]

Dear fellow people, does it still taste good to you?!

Another worker reported:

> *A lot of times the skinner finds out an animal is still conscious when he slices the side of its head and it starts kicking wildly. … then the skinners shove a knife into the back of its head to cut the spinal cord.*
>
> *After the head-skinner, the carcass proceeds to the leggers, … "As far as the ones that come back to life," says a line worker, … "it looks like they're trying to climb the wall. … And when they get to the leggers, well, the leggers don't want to start working on the cow until somebody gets down there to reknock it. So they just cut off the bottom part of the leg with the clippers. When they do that, the cattle go wild, just kicking in every direction."*
>
> *The animal then proceeds to be … and cut in half, at which point it finally looks like the stereotyped image of beef…*[50]

> can we leave out comment: **Well**, bon appétit …

Here we can only say: Bon appétit, enjoy your meal!

And a worker reports about slaughtering pigs:
> *Down in the blood pit they say that the smell of blood makes you aggressive. And it does. You get an attitude that …you're already going to kill the hog, but that's not enough. It has to suffer. … You go in hard, push hard, blow the windpipe, make it drown in its own blood. Split its nose. … cut its eye out … One time I took my knife … and I sliced off the end of a hog's nose …*[51] etc., etc.

Dear reader, does it still taste good?!

> *When Temple Grandin first began to quantify the scale of abuse in slaughterhouses, she reported witnessing "deliberate acts of cruelty occurring on a regular basis" at 32 percent of the plants she surveyed during announced visits in the United States.*[52]

But what happens when no inspections are announced beforehand, that is, when the operators had no time to clean up the worst abuses?

Jonathan S. Foer concludes:
> *Human beings cannot be human (much less humane) under the conditions of a factory farm or slaughterhouse.*[53]

In the German newspaper DIE ZEIT from Feb. 23, 2012, Gunhild Lütke writes as follows in the article "The Butchers" about slaughtering pigs:

In big slaughterhouses they – the pigs – *glide into the depths in gondolas. The pit is filled with a gas that numbs the animals. Back above, they are tipped out and hung up. A stab in the neck ensures that they bleed out, which leads to death. Usually. Sometimes the animals die an especially agonizing death, because they don't bleed properly. Then, still alive, they go into the scalder, which sees to it that the upper skin layer and bristles can be removed. But sometimes, already with the numbing things don't work right.*

Shall we still wish a bon appétit?

The article continues:
Already years ago, Professor Klaus Tröger of the Max-Rubner-Institute pilloried the animal torture in many slaughterhouses. …
Studies have found that approximately 500,000 pigs are scalded alive every year. And with 200,000 cattle, the first bolt shot meant to anaesthetize doesn't work, so that these animals have to be shot several times, which, nevertheless, doesn't lead to a lasting numbing.

Although meanwhile, the situation is supposed to have improved, it's reported that as before,
> it's not precluded that pigs are scalded alive because they don't bleed out properly. When you then hear them in the tunnel, where in modern plants the steam scalding takes place, banging against the wall from the pain, it's a gruesome thing.

Further from "Die Zeit" of Feb. 23, 2012:
> The precarious phase begins for the animals when they come out of the numbing area. Then they are hung up and transported a few meters to the stabber. However, mostly he doesn't see if enough blood is flowing out so that the animals are really dead. It's not rare that a single worker stabs 750 pigs – in an hour! So he has only a few seconds to place the cut properly. It can also happen that a stabber overlooks a pig. Then it, too, lands in the scalding machine alive.

As cruelly as the life of a hog ends, it begins just as cruelly.
An article by Georg Entscheid, entitled "The Hog Farmer" in the same newspaper DIE ZEIT, also from Feb. 23, 2012. He describes what happens to newborn male piglets:

Male piglets go through a special procedure. A worker grabs one by its hind legs. Then two cuts with a knife in the pale pink skin, where the testicles are concealed. The at most 7-days-old animal screams pitifully. The seminal ducts have to be cut with a razorblade, but sometimes the thin strands are simply torn off. It has to go fast. Time is money. The wound remains open. Only now is the piglet injected with something that should relieve the wound pain for a few hours. But its torments have not yet ended. In a second run his ringtail is cut off with a hot knife and his eyeteeth are worked on with a grinding machine. Both are meant to prevent the animals from biting off each other's tails. They tend to do this because they can't live out their natural behavior in the monotonous huge barns designed for maximum efficiency.

The suffering described here in brief words is inflicted on the animals every minute, every hour, every day, in barns, in slaughter plants all over the world. Now, at this moment, while you read this book, or in the moment, in which you play with your children, or you enjoy your grandchildren, while you work, while you sleep – unceasingly, this cruel, bestial behavior toward our fellow creatures in barns everywhere is taking place.

It says further in the article by Georg Entscheid:
For the German Minister of Agriculture, Ilse Aigner, however, every new barn is a success. The politician of the Christian Democratic Union wants to make Germany a leading meat-export nation, which can compete with providers like Brazil and the USA.

With the political parties that call themselves Christian, the "C" stands for Christian. However, before the background of the just-described animal suffering, this "C" is a mockery of the Christ of God and of all His fellow creatures. It is scorn and derision of the name of Jesus of Nazareth, the Christ of God! That, too, is Germany.

Anyone who wants to inform himself further can do this extensively in Internet. Animal protection organizations and vegetarian sites, facts about hunting, the fur industry and factory farming show the horror more than clearly.

By the way: Being an animal friend and eating animals is mutually exclusive. Many true animal friends are vegetarians or vegans and have left the church long ago because of the doctrinal statements of the churches concerning nature and animals. And their example is encouraging; yes, it calls to others: Don't look away. Look at what's being done to the animals – billionfold. Eat no meat! Do not eat the suffering of the animals!

**Catholic and Protestant-Lutheran:
Mockery and derision of Jesus
and of His teaching *for* the life**

Jesus, the Christ, says:
> *Verily, I say to you, I Am come into the world in order to put an end to all blood offerings and to the eating of the flesh of animals and birds that are slain by men.*

Jesus, the Christ, also essentially said: Teach first, then baptize. But apparently for reasons of purely political power, the churches have reversed the teaching of Jesus of Nazareth. Now it is: First baptize the under-age baby – under threat of eternal damnation for the parents in case they don't have their child baptized – then teach the child, or the growing youth, the fear of eternal damnation. And further: Give them meat to eat; do away with their inherent disgust of the cadaver meal as soon as possible. The result is that babies are already presently being fed puréed animal-carcass. – Jesus of Nazareth did not teach this!

Already back then, Jesus of Nazareth spoke a very clear language to many people of the folk, but above all, to the caste of priests:

Why do you not understand what I say? It is because you cannot bear to hear my word. You are of your father the devil, and your will is to do your father's desires. He was a murderer from the beginning, and does not stand in the truth, because there is no truth in him. When he lies, he speaks out of his own character, for he is a liar and the father of lies. But because I tell the truth, you do not believe me. … If I tell the truth, why do you not believe me? Whoever is of God hears the words of God. The reason why you do not hear them is that you are not of God. (Joh 8:43-47)

What is it like today?

When we hear these clear words spoken with authority by the courageous man Jesus of Nazareth, then we know why the caste of priests had Him killed. What would they do today?

Let us realize that the step-by-step fulfillment of the Sermon on the Mount in relation to nature and the animals could have prevented the downfall of mankind via the climate change. But with 2000 years of leading the nations astray, today mankind is standing at the edge of the abyss as never before. In reality, it is even over the edge of the abyss; we're merely counting time until it hits bottom! This is said today by well-known scientists such as James Lovelock, Frank Fenner and Gwynne Dyer.

This is clearly the result of the institutional, allegedly Christian, church doctrine, of the egoistical striving for power by a caste of priests that, in truth, have repeatedly despised, even fought against, and continue to do so until today, the born life and the teachings of the Christ of God, whose name is on their lips until today.

In contrast, individual courageous women and men tried again and again to enlighten the people. This was done through "great personalities," who, despite all resistance by the churches, clearly and plainly pointed out what the true "values" of the churches are. It is their deeds. Let us realize that every bit of progress in the history of mankind was always won *against* the influence of the churches.

When have the churches ever championed the interests of the people or of nature and the animals?

History teaches us the opposite, namely, that always and exclusively with the respective ruling powers of an epoch, the churches indoctrinated, exploited and oppressed the people – and that, until today. And most people nevertheless find it very normal that until today these churches are allowed to call themselves "Christian," even though nearly everyone knows that Jesus of Nazareth taught something entirely different than what the churches have made of it with fire and sword, with lies and deception, over the course of history. Only because the good name of "Jesus of Nazareth," that is, the name "Christian," is not legally protected. However, interestingly enough, the names "Catholic" and "Lutheran" are indeed legally protected.

Great personalities in world history denounce the murder of animals

We could present a long list of names of famous personalities and their charges against the Church and the murder of animals, and we want to name just a few. They are: Johann Wolfgang von Goethe, Immanuel Kant, Frederick the Great, Francois Voltaire, Heinrich Böll, Albert Schweitzer, Heinrich

Heine, Leo Tolstoy, Napoleon, Karlheinz Deschner, Friedrich Nietzsche and many, many more.

Many of the so-called "great minds," personalities of world fame, spoke specifically for the animals and against the murder of animals.

In the following, several quotations by these great personalities:

Whoever leaves the church is a ray of hope for me; whoever no longer eats animals is my brother. (Karlheinz Deschner[54])

Wherever a person takes the right to sacrifice an animal for a purpose, he not only commits a wrong, but a crime. (Karlheinz Deschner[55])

After intensely studying the history of Christianity, I know of no organization in antiquity, in the Middle Ages and during the present times, including and especially the 20th century, that at the same time is so long, so continuously and so terribly burdened with crime as is the Christian Church, particularly the Roman-Catholic Church (Karlheinz Deschner [56])

The mass murder of the animals for the consumption of meat is today nothing but cannibalism, modified by one degree. The whole world groans under turmoil, disease and mismanagement – but can a person demand that things go well for him, when he himself desecrates nature and practices the most abominable cruelties day after day on millions of defenseless creatures? (Manfred Kyber[57])

The misery of man will last as long as the lamentation of animals cries out to heaven. (Manfred Kyber[58])

There are many absurdities in the propositions of the church, but nevertheless rule it will, so it must have a narrow-minded multitude, which bows its head and likes to be ruled. The high and richly endowed clergy dread nothing more than the enlightenment of the lower orders ... (Johann Wolfgang von Goethe[59])

Can there be anything more abominable than to constantly nourish oneself from the flesh of carcasses? (Francois Voltaire[60])

The narrow gate and the strait path that leads to life is that of the good moral conduct; the wide gate and the broad path that many take is the church. (Immanuel Kant[61])

Instinct continues to be the explanation of choice whenever animal behavior implies too much intelligence (Jonathan Safran Foer[62])

Allow me to say that our present religions are as little like the [religion] of Christ as that of the Iroquois. ... Jesus preached tolerance and we persecute. Jesus preached a good moral doctrine and we do not practice it. Jesus did not establish dogmas; the councils however have richly seen to that. In short: A Christian of the third century is not at all similar to a Christian of the first century anymore. (Fredrick the Great[63])

If there were no such state religion, no preemption of a dogma and a cult, then Germany would be united and strong, and her sons would be glorious and free. But this way, our poor fatherland is torn by religious conflict, the folk is divided into hostile religious parties ... everywhere mistrust ... everywhere denunciation, espionage to determine sympathies ... church-newspaper snoopery, sect hate, proselytism, and while we argue about heaven, we perish on Earth! (Heinrich Heine[64])

It will be a great advance in the development of the human race when we become fruit eaters and the meat eaters disappear from the Earth. Everything will become possible on our planet starting from the moment when we overcome the bloody meals of flesh and overcome war. (George Sand[65])

Theology in religion is what poisons are in food. (Napoleon[66])

In its average organ, German Catholicism is rotten to the point of being dirty, and in its methods, dumb to the point of being brazen. (Heinrich Böll[67])

What can we expect from a religion when we exclude compassion for animals? (Richard Wagner[68])

Anyone who thinks he is a Christian because he goes to church, is wrong. Going to church doesn't make you a Christian any more than going to the garage makes you a car. (Albert Schweitzer[69])

Reverence for life means abhorrence of killing.
Wherever an animal is forced into the service of man, the suffering it endures concerns us all. (Albert Schweitzer[70])

When you read the legends of its saints, you find the names of a thousand canonized criminals. (C. A. Helvetius[71])

I condemn Christianity; I bring against the Christian church the most terrible of all the accusations that an accuser has ever had in his mouth. It is, to me, the greatest of all imaginable corruptions; … it has turned every value into worthlessness, and every truth into a lie, and every integrity into baseness of soul. Let anyone dare to speak to me of its "humanitarian" blessings! Its deepest necessities range it against any effort to abolish distress; it lives by distress; it creates distress to make itself immortal …
I call Christianity the one great curse, the one great intrinsic depravity, the one great instinct of revenge, for which no means are venomous enough, or secret, subterranean and small enough – I call it the one immortal blemish upon the human race. … (Friedrich Nietzsche[72])

So there we have it: A church order with priesthood, theologians, cults, sacraments, in short, everything that Jesus of Nazareth fought against … (Friedrich Nietzsche[73])

A true human culture will only exist when not only human gluttony, but all eating of meat is considered cannibalism. (Wilhelm Busch[74])

No matter how badly the governors of God acted, the besotted people didn't open their stupid eyes. Princes and people let themselves be milked by these revolting villians and for this they still humbly kissed the tyrants slippers. (Otto von Corvin[75])

If anyone wants to save the planet, all they have to do is just stop eating meat. (Paul McCartney[76])

It is possible that mankind is on the threshold of a golden age; but, if so, it will be necessary first to slay the dragon that guards the door, and this dragon is religion. (Bertrand Russell[77])

… the primary task of religion is to prevent any psychic independence on the part of the people, to intimidate them intellectually, to bring them into the socially necessary infantile docility toward the authorities. (Erich Fromm[78])

Dear reader, what do you think? – Why did and do so many great thinkers and philosophers, artists, statesmen and scientists, the spiritually elite of the people, write about the churches and about the animals in such a straightforward manner? Why do we celebrate their birthdays and yet, do not think about what values they stood for?

Mass murder of people, mass murder of animals: An enormous guilt, measured by the spiritual-cosmic laws

Many people know or sense, but often suppress, that thoughtless consumption may imply complicity, a share in the blame, for instance, in the crimes against nature and animals. Thus, many people are not necessarily the main perpetrators of a crime against nature, but many do indeed share in contributing to the suffering of the animals, because, for example, they, as tag-alongs, eat pieces of animal carcasses.

Many a person will say: "I live my life largely within the law." We don't want to deny this of anyone. But we ask: Does that which is allowed by the legal system of the individual countries and states also measure up to the spiritual-cosmic standards?
For example, the Ten Commandments of God through Moses and the Sermon on the Mount of Jesus of Nazareth? If we compare our life, our way of thinking, speaking and acting, with the Ten Commandments of God through Moses and the Sermon on the Mount of Jesus of Nazareth, then are we still so sure of ourselves in the statement: "I live my life largely within the law"?

Let us not fool ourselves. Many people are aware of their bad conscience. But when, despite the billion-fold appalling suffering and the bestial brutality – for example, in factory farming and animal testing – a person no longer has pangs of conscience, has he not then lost his conscience? Has not the person become someone without a conscience in this point? It appears that many people should be placed into this category. If with all the suffering and misery, the cruelty and bestiality toward the animals and toward people, a person's heart is not stirred, isn't he then heartless?

Can we truly say that we love our children and grandchildren when it has been determined that with every animal we eat, the future of our children and grandchildren worsens?

At this point, we want to present a statement by Jean Ziegler, for many years UN Special Rapporteur on the Right to Food. He said:

Why did I become a vegetarian?
For many reasons: Once, I was sick and the new diet cured me. Therefore I stayed with it. Secondly: The worldwide grain harvest is about 2 billion tons a year. Over 500 million tons are fed to the livestock of the

rich nations – while, according to UN statistics, in the 122 countries of the Third World, 43,000 children die of hunger every day.

I no longer want to be part of this dreadful mass murder. Not to eat meat is a minimal beginning. (Jean Ziegler[79])

[Editor's Note: The above is written as our source quotes Mr. Ziegler. However, recent sources show that it is more like 760 million tons that are fed to animals.[80]]

Nearly 40 million people die annually of hunger or its immediate results[81]; that's more than 100,000 people per day – truly a horrible mass murder! But the immeasurable suffering of the animals through meat production is condoned by the churches, and factory farming is not only tolerated by church functionaries and politicians who call themselves Christian, but obviously promoted. The horrible worldwide negative effects of meat consumption, above all, for the people of the Third World, are apparently accepted by the churches. This is Catholic and Protestant-Lutheran. Jesus of Nazareth did not teach such a thing.

Perhaps many people are now thinking that these hideous crimes committed on people, nature and animals are being addressed somewhat "too clearly," above all, in terms of the great share of guilt of the churches in this. Many a one may perhaps think: "Psst, not too loud, please, even though you're right! And besides, Bishop XY is otherwise a nice guy." – Is he really?

Can anyone be a nice guy who remains silent about injustice and crimes, yes, even knowingly condones them? And when, on top of that, he merely drapes the cloak "Christian" around himself and continuously deceives the folk? A leading figure in a church, in particular, should first of all keep the Ten Commandments of God and the Sermon on the Mount of Jesus of Nazareth as a standard for his life. Anything else is a betrayal of the Nazarene, Jesus, the Christ – if one calls oneself "Christian."

Apparently, as Catholic or Lutheran or some other kind of Protestant, one has different standards, namely, those that are not Christian. Then one can seem nice for those that want to have things this way and for those who are satisfied with this. With this, one believes it's possible to sweep all the indicated injustice under the carpet.

Aside from the fact that Jesus of Nazareth did not appoint any priests to His following – as is generally known from the history of the Church – what about the function of the leading figures of the Church as role models, particularly in terms of vegetarianism and climate change?

Every child meanwhile knows that eating meat is one of the main causes of climate disaster. In the book "Was Bischöfen schmeckt,"[82] ("What Tastes Good to Bishops,") however, we can read that almost all bishops prefer to eat animal carcass pieces. The whole range of dead animals lands on the bishops' table. That is their function as role models in terms of animal suffering and climate collapse.
The church leaders can act as they wish, but then they should not call themselves Christian, because Jesus and His followers as well as the people in the first communities did not eat meat.

But let's ask the question: Why are the words of God through prophets not taken seriously by the leading figures of the churches – especially by their highest dignitaries – and why are the teachings of Jesus of Nazareth obviously betrayed?
Why were the vegetarian apostles Peter, Paul and others and even Jesus, the Christ, excommunicated by the Catholic Church as "godless heretics"?

Why, instead, are the words of priests and Doctors of the Church – according to today's standard, often malicious word-twisters, even criminals such as Thomas of Aquinas, Augustine, Constantine and Pope John III – raised to be the standard for over 1 billion institutional "Christians"? Why? Each one can answer this for himself.

**Vegetarians, the "godless heretics" –
still eternally damned by the Church.
Who is the father of lies?**

Let us realize that the Catholic Church teaches the following:
All vegetarians on Earth are still "godless heretics" and damned eternally, because the Doctor of the Church Augustine, the "saint," wanted it this way – the special "friend" of Ratzinger, of whom, according to his own words, former Pope Ratzinger requests support and help. For according to the doctrine of Augustine, vegetarianism is, until today, "a godless heretical concept."

Let us also realize that the Catholic Church teaches the following: At the first Synod of Braga in the year

561, Pope John III, 561-574, declared all vegetarians to be excommunicated with the following:

If anyone considers the foods of the flesh unclean, which God has given for the use of men … but … so abstains from these … let him be anathema.[83]

Let us also become aware that in "The Teaching of the Catholic Church" by Neuner and Roos, we find under Margin Note 78, and I quote:

Any one does not accept the whole of the Church's tradition, both written and unwritten – anathema sit.

According to church doctrine, this means eternal damnation for all vegetarians worldwide. For all eternity! Why? Because vegetarians let animals live and don't kill them to afterward eat them up, that is, pardon the expression, devour them.

For people who kill, rob, murder, plunder and have to answer for the billionfold animal massacre, heaven remains open – according to the Catechism and dogma – for it says: A quick confession before death, receive the "last rites," and you're off to the Catholic heaven.

Isn't that quite obviously satanic? It can hardly be clearer. Anyone who protects life lands in eternal damnation. On the other hand, anyone who avails himself of the Catholic "instant redemption" in the form of the sacraments goes to the Catholic heaven. That's the Catholic pattern.

But God, the Eternal, the All-love, did not give people meat dishes to eat. Eating meat belongs to the passions of those people who have attributed the alleged permission for this to God, the All-life. This is the lying and falsification by the caste of priests, like so unendingly much more is also pure falsification and presumption, in order to keep the people dependent. But who is the father of lies?

Let it be repeated once more: Being an animal friend and eating animals is mutually exclusive, and many true animal friends are therefore also vegetarians or vegans and have turned away from the Church and its doctrine that despises nature.

The animal friends say: Don't look away. Look at what's being done to the animals – billionfold. Eat no meat! Do not eat the suffering of the animals!! Eating meat is truly against the law of life, which is God.

As things look now, the war of extermination against life on Earth will end only when the climate collapse shows the monster – the beast, man – the limits, in that mankind perishes in the most ghastly way through manmade worldwide apocalyptic disasters, that is, it destroys itself, and all that, just within a few decades.

The Third World War has already begun. Where is the way out?

But we are already living in a world of abysmal inequality and advancing impoverishment – in the western world everything is under the ethical-moral leadership of the stinking rich, so-called Christian churches. Every day over 1 billion people go hungry and more than 100,000 people die of hunger or its immediate consequences,[84] because, among other things, the rich industrial nations feed the grain to their cattle herds in factory farming. Whereby it is known that it takes 16 kg of grain to produce 1 kg of meat.
We feed so much grain to animals, in order to fatten them up for consumption, that, if we all would become vegetarians, we could produce more than enough food to feed the entire world population. In truth, this is and remains the sole way for mankind to survive on this Earth.

Jean Ziegler, vegetarian and, for many years UN Special Rapporteur on the Right to Food, wrote already in 2002:

> *The four Apocalyptic Riders of under-development are Famine, Thirst, Epidemic and War, killing more men, women and children every year than the slaughter of WW2 did in six years. For the people of the Third World, World War III is already in full swing …*
> *Year after year, hundreds of millions of severely malnourished mothers bring hundreds of millions of terminally damaged babies into the world.*
> *Those who have the money eat and live; those who have none go hungry, become an invalid or die.*[85]

> *30 million people starve annually; hundreds of millions die of the consequences of illness and disease, epidemics and deficiencies as a result of undernourishment. Tens of thousands of people go blind every year due to malnutrition.*[86]

The church campaigns for the *unborn* life. Is this because it still wants to baptize it, thus later ensuring its sinecures? But why is the life that has already been *born* disregarded everywhere – be it human, nature or animal – is it worthless?

Apparently, people may well be used as cannon fodder in war; they can starve to death or die of Aids; nature can be destroyed and animals murdered in droves. Apparently the churches have no problem with this. All this can be blessed.

The churches' problem is the "unborn life." Here they talk about "ethics" and "morals," thus diverting attention from the immeasurable wealth of the churches, for instance. The ethics and morals of the institutional, allegedly Christian church leaders are demonstrated by the fact that they call for "ethics" and "morals" in everything and everyone, but mostly remain silent when it comes to protecting "born" life. For instance, they remain silent in order to protect clerical child abusers from criminal prosecution and to evade secular jurisdiction. And they remain silent when it's all about ensuring their own sinecures. But their silence does not satisfy the hunger and suffering of this world.

Why do the immeasurably rich churches, which have snatched up hundreds of billions over the course of history, hardly give from their wealth for the suffering, for the poor, and instead, always demand that others give?

What they perhaps do give – but only perhaps – are not even bread crumbs, not even the oft-cited "drop in the bucket."

Is that the teaching of Jesus of Nazareth? No. He said:

> *… it is easier for a camel to go through the eye of a needle than for a rich person to enter the kingdom of God.*

So it's no wonder that more and more people are fleeing in droves from church stone buildings – where they mostly hear only hollow phrases anyway – and take seriously the words of John, the seer of Patmos, who said:

> *Come out of her, my people, lest you take part in her sins, lest you share in her plagues.* (Rev. 18:4)

Everyone should believe whatever he wants to. Let the people in the institutional churches call themselves Catholic, or Lutheran, or whatever. That would at least be honest, because the institutional churches, as well as the so-called Christian political parties, don't have the slightest bit to do with Jesus of Nazareth, but indeed with the immeasurable suffering of people, nature and animals on this maltreated Earth. So, why do the churches and C-parties call themselves Christian when it's so very obvious that they serve another power? They could call themselves Lutheran or Catholic or whatever, then everyone can recognize what's really going on!

Followers of Jesus of Nazareth are for His rehabilitation. They believe in the words of the Christ of God, who, according to apocryphal scriptures, spoke very clear words – also for the animals and against the consumption of meat – for example, in "The Gospel of The Holy Twelve," also known as the "The Gospel of Perfect Life" or the "Gospel of Jesus," that is outside of the Bible. Jesus spoke:

But I say to you: Shed no innocent blood and eat no flesh. Be upright, love mercy and do right, and your days will endure in the land for a long time. (Chap. 33:8)

And He also admonished:

Woe to the hunters! For they themselves shall be hunted! (Chap. 14:7)

And He said:

Is it not written that, in the beginning, God ordained the fruits of the trees and the seeds and the plants to be food for all flesh? (Chap. 33:6)

Also passed down in the "Gospel of the Holy Twelve":

And some of the people said, "This man takes care of all the animals. Are they His brothers and sisters, that He loves them so?" And He said to them, "Verily, these are your fellow brothers from the great family of God, your brothers and sisters who have the same breath of life from the Eternal.

And whoever cares for the least of them and gives it food and drink in its need does this to Me, and the one who deliberately allows that one of them suffer privation and does not defend it when it is ill-treated allows this evil to happen as if it were done to Me. For just as you have done in this life will it be done to you in the life to come." (Chap. 34:9-10)

Jesus of Nazareth made it unmistakably clear:
God gives the grains and the fruits of the Earth as food; and for the righteous man, there is no other lawful nourishment for the body. (Chap. 38:3)

Let us remember that the animals are our little brothers and sisters. Animals, all animals, also have social contact among each other. Animals love their children and care for them. Animals can mourn; animals express joy; animals are animate beings; they have a consciousness; animals cultivate deep friendships; animals have the finest sensory perception, which lets them feel the bestial behavior of people toward them all the more.

Animals are intelligent – all of them, without exception! Animals, too, have a soul or a part-soul, which lives on after they pass on. And many animals would have a life expectancy of many decades if the beast man wouldn't murder them already during earliest childhood, in order to devour them! Yes, you read correctly: The flesh of the murdered animals is primarily the flesh of animal children!

Jesus, the Christ, speaks:
Verily, I say to you, I Am come into the world in order to put an end to all blood offerings and to the eating of the flesh of animals and birds that are slain by men.
In the beginning, God gave everyone the fruits of the trees and the seeds and the herbs for food; but those who loved themselves more than God or their neighbor corrupted their ways and brought diseases into their bodies and filled the Earth with lust and cruelty. Not by shedding innocent blood, but by living a righteous life, will you find the peace of God.

You call Me the Christ of God and you speak true; for I Am the way, the truth and the life. Walk this way, and you will find God. Seek the truth, and the truth will make you free. (Gospel of the Holy Twelve, Chap. 74:9-12)

I wish to all my fellowmen the freedom in God, the free Spirit of love, and the unity of man, nature and animals. The truth that makes us free is that the church laws, the rites, dogmas and priest cults, the churches of stone with all their content are made by man and have not the least bit to do with Jesus of Nazareth. God is in us, in each person, in each soul – that is what Jesus of Nazareth taught us. *That* is the truth that makes us free.

At all times, God, the Eternal, sent prophetesses and prophets to the people. God, the Eternal, sent no priests and no pope. God, the Eternal, sent Jesus, the Christ, to us people. He taught us the spiritual principles of the Sermon on the Mount, for us to fulfill them in our daily life. Everything else is the work of man.

Dear reader, much, very much has been clearly addressed and expressed here. The suffering of the animals is so indescribably cruel, that one simply may not remain silent. No one, really no one, is meant to be personally discredited or pilloried here, who, in all conscience, simply lives his life as he feels is correct. But followers of Jesus of Nazareth repudiate the fact that this bestial behavior against the creatures of God is committed by many people under the abuse of the name of Jesus of Nazareth.

It remains to be hoped that with these lines perhaps a further door could open up for the animals in many a heart.

When we see animals, let us remember that they are our little brothers and sisters in the great creation of God. Let us look deeply into their eyes more often. It is God, the Eternal, the All-love, which is radiating to us through our animal brothers and sisters: "I Am in everything and everyone – also in the animal."

Sources

1. Protocol German Parliament, 14th election period, 237th session. May 17, 2002.
2. Ouseley, G.J. *The Gospel of the Holy Twelve*, Newly edited by Udny, E. F., Printed and published by Edson (Printers) Limited, London, 1923.
3. *Pseudo-Clementines* XII, http://en.wikipedia.org/wiki/Christian_vegetarianism
4. Krauss, Samuel. *Toledoth Jeschu*, Berlin 1920, p. 113, quoted from Carl Anders Skriver, *Die Lebensweise Jesu und der ersten Christen* 2nd ed., Bad Bellingen, 1988, p. 121.
5. *Paedogogus II:1*; http://www.newadvent.org/fathers/2092.htm
6. Eusebius. *History of the Church II 2:3*
7. Augustine. *Epistulae ad Faustum XXII, 3*
8. Tertullian. *Apology*, Chap. 9; http://www.intratext.com/IXT/ENG2035/_PD.HTM
9. Carl Anders Skriver. *Die vergessenen Anfänge der Schöpfung und des Christentums*, Lübeck 1977, p. 123.
10. Carl Anders Skriver, *Stephanus, die nazoräische Botschaft*, p. 22.
11. Robert Springer. *Enkarpa, Kulturgeschichte der Menschheit im Lichte der pythagoräischen Lehre*, Hannover, 1884, p. 288 ff.
12. Homily 69
13. Pliny the Younger. Epistulae Lib. X, 96.
14. Jerome. *Against Jovinianus, Book I, no. 18.* http://www.ccel.org/ccel/schaff/npnf206.vi.vi.I.html
15. Mynarek, H. *Papst Entzauberung*, Books on Demand, 2007, p. 18.
16. Seewald, P. Benedict XVI, *Light of the World*, Libreria Editrice Vaticana, Vatican City, 2010, p. 17.
17. Deschner, K., *Kriminalgeschichte des Christentums*, Vol. I, p. 486
18. *Ibid.*, p. 486f.
19. *Ibid.*, p. 517f.
20. Augustine, *City of God, Book 1, chap. 20.* http://www.newadvent.org/fathers/120101.htm

[21] *Ibid.*
[22] Augustine, *Tractate on the Gospel of John*, 1:18, http://www.newadvent.org/fathers/1701001.htm
[23] Neuner, J. & Roos H. *The Teaching of the Catholic Church, Margin Note 103*, Mercier Press, Ltd., 1967
[24] Thomas of Aquinas, Summa Contra Gentiles, Book 2, chap. 82:6. http://dhspriory.org/thomas/ContraGentiles2.htm#82
[25] Aquinas. *Summa theologica II* .64.1. http://www.newadvent.org/summa/3064.htm
[26] *Ibid*. II.25.3. http://www.ccel.org/ccel/aquinas/summa.SS_Q25_A3.html
[27] *Ibid:* II.64.3. http://www.newadvent.org/summa/3064.htm
[28] *Ibid.* II.64.1. http://www.newadvent.org/summa/3064.htm
[29] Denzinger, H. and Schönmetzer, A. *Enchiridion symbolorum definitionum et declarationum de rebus fidei et morum.* Freiburg, Herder, 1991, p. 140. English translation: http://denzinger.patristica.net/ (244.14).
[30] Deschner, K. *ob. cit.*, Vol. 1, p. 213.
[31] Aquinas, *Summa theologica I.92*.art. 1. reply to objection 1. http://www.newadvent.org/summa/1092.htm
[32] Paul Graf von Hoensbroech. *Das Papsttum in seiner sozial-kulturellen Wirksamkeit,* Leipzig, 1904, p. 35.
[33] Bejick, Urte. *Die Katharerinnen*, Freiburg, 1993, p. 42.
[34] Deschner, K. Opus diaboli, Hamburg, 1989, p. 28.
[35] Saarbrücken, 2009, p. 45.
[36] Foer, J. S. *Eating Animals*. Back Bay Books / Little, Brown and Company, New York, NY, 2009, p. 34.
[37] *Ibid.*, p. 33.
[38] *Ibid.*, p. 35.
[39] *Ibid.*, p. 65.
[40] Bavarian Broadcasting program: *Summit Meeting.* Nov. 1, 2009.
[41] *This Is My Word. Alpha and Omega. The Gospel of Jesus. The Christ-Revelation which True Christians the World Over Have Come to Know*. The Word – The Universal Spirit in Universal Life, Woodbridge, CT, USA, 4th ed., 2011.

[42] Augustine, *City of God*, Book 1, chap. 20. http://www.newadvent.org/fathers/120101.htm
[43] Foer, J. S., *ob cit.*, pp. 255-256.
[44] *Ibid.*, p. 55.
[45] *Ibid.*, pp. 64-65.
[46] *Ibid.*, p. 229.
[47] *Ibid.*, p. 230.
[48] *Ibid.*, p. 231.
[49] *Ibid.*, p. 231.
[50] *Ibid.*, p. 233.
[51] *Ibid.*, p. 253.
[52] *Ibid.*, p. 255.
[53] *Ibid.*, p. 256.
[54] Deschner, K. *Nurnberger Nachrichten*, Dec. 7, 2011.
[55] Deschner, K. *Für einen Bissen Fleisch*, p. 10.
[56] Deschner, K. *Die beleidigte Kirche*, Freiburg, 1986, p. 42f.
[57] Kyber, M. *Weiße Fahne*, 12/1931.
[58] Kyber, M. cited from Armin Risi, Ronald Zürrer, *Vegetarisch Leben*, Zürich 2011.
[59] Von Goethe, J. W., from Eckermann, J.P., *Conversations of Goethe with Johann Peter Eckermann*. (Translator's note. This quote obtained by "Look Inside" book on sale by Amazon, an unabridged replication of the version published in London in 1930)
[60] Voltaire, F. cited from Risi/Zürrer, p. 81.
[61] Kant, I. Die Religion innerhalb der Grenzen der Bloßen Vernunft, Stuttgart, 1986, p. 75.
[62] Foer, J. S., *ob cit.*, p. 64.
[63] Friedrich der Große und die Philosophie, Texte und Dokumente, Bernhard H. F. Taureck (pub.) Stuttgart 1986, p. 75.
[64] Heine, H. Reisebilder, Vol. 4, Hamburg, 1834, p. 106f.
[65] Sand, G. cited from Risi/Zürrer, p. 84.
[66] Napoleon, http://www.lifequoteslib.com/quotes theology.html
[67] Böll, H. *Warum so zartfühlend?*, *Der Spiegel*, May 15, 1967.
[68] Wagner, R. cited from Skriver, C. A. *Die Lebensweise Jesus und der ersten Christen*, Bad Bellingen, 1988, p. 136.

[69] Schweitzer, A. http://www.unmoralische.de/athe_3.htm
[70] Schweitzer, A. cited from Risi/Zürrer, p. 90.
[71] Helvetius, C. A. cited from Deschner, K. *Die Politik der Päpste im 20. Jahrhundert*, Hamburg, 1991, p. 13.
[72] Nietzsche, F. (http://www.gutenberg.org/files/19322/19322-h/19322-h.htm (The Antichrist, no 62).
[73] Nietzsche, F. *Kritische Studienausgabe*, 1999, *Nachlass*, p. 116.
[74] Busch, W. http://www.animaladvocates.com/animal-quotes/
[75] Von Corvin, O. *Pfaffenspiegel*, Schwerte, 1980, p. 119.
[76] McCartney, P. http://www.examiner.com/article/quotes-by-paul-mccartney-about-vegetarianism
[77] Russell, B. http://thinkexist.com/quotation/it_is_possible_that_mankind_is_on_the_threshold/ 172898.html
[78] Fromm, E. http://www.erich-fromm.de/data/pdf/Funk,The%20Courage%20to%20Be%20Human.pdf p.85
[79] Ziegler, J., Letter to the authors of the book by Armin Risi and Ronald Zürrer, *Vegetarisch Leben*, Zürich, 2006, p. 46. www.provegan.info/eng/vegan/for-human-rights/seite-2/
[80] www.earth-policy.org/data_highlights/2011/highlights22 http://evolvecampaigns.org.uk/evolve/famine.aspx
[81] Ziegler, J. *Hamburger Abendblatt*, Jan. 20, 2006.
[82] Knörzer, H. and Kuric, I. *Was Bischöfen Schmeckt*, Baurer-Verlag, Thalhofen.
[83] Denzinger, H. and Schönmetzer, A. *Enchiridion symbolorum definitionum et declarationum de rebus fidei et morum*. Freiburg, Herder, 1991, p. 140. English translation: http://denzinger.patristica.net/(244.14).
[84] Ziegler, J. *Hamburger Abendblatt*, Jan. 20, 2006.
[85] Ziegler, J. *Die neuen Herrscher der Welt*, Munich, 2003, p. 13f.

Sources and other informative literature

Jonathan Safran Foer: "Eating Animals", Back Bay Books / Little, Brown and Company, New York

Gabriele: "You, the Animal – You, the Human Being. Which Has Higher Values?", Universal Life – The Inner Religion

"This Is My Word. Alpha and Omega",
The Word – The Universal Spirit in Universal Life

"The Animal-Friendly Cookbook. On the Way to Nature",
The Word – The Universal Spirit in Universal Life

"The Hidden Love of Jesus For the Animals",
The Word – The Universal Spirit in Universal Life

Gabriele: "Animals Lament – The Prophet Denounces",
The Word – The Universal Spirit in Universal Life

Gabriele: "The Murder of Animals Is The Death of Human Beings", The Word – The Universal Spirit in Universal Life

"What Has Eyes Intelligent People Do Not Eat",
The Word – The Universal Spirit in Universal Life

Mariana Georgacarakos: "Animal Rights and Cruelty Including Anti-Hunting, Factory Farming, Animal Testing, Animal Laws, and Animal Rights Cases", Apr 18, 2011

Peter Singer: "In Defense of Animals: The Second Wave", Wiley Desktop Editions, Sep 5, 2005

www.peta.org

http://www.albertschweitzerfoundation.org/

www.earthwatch.org

www.veg.soc.org

JESUS, THE CHRIST, ALSO CAME FOR THE ANIMALS

This Is My Word
Alpha and Omega
The Gospel of Jesus
The Christ-Revelation, Which True Christians the World Over Have Come to Know

Jesus was a man of the people – not of the churches! Learn until now unknown details about the life and the teaching of Jesus, the Christ. Throughout the work, „This Is My Word," His teaching draws through the pages like a common thread to the people: To respect and to love nature and the animals. For example:

Christ also Came to Deliver the Animals from Their Suffering and Torment! – Respect for the Life of the Plants and Animals – Jesus Reproaches Cruelty Against a Horse – The One Who Lives in God Is One with All Creatures – The Extinction of Many Animal Species – The Meaning of Many Animals for an Ecological Balance – The Law of Sowing and Reaping also Applies in Dealings with Creation – Animal Sacrifice and Eating Meat – Animal Experiments Are an Abomination to God – Food, a Gift of God – Diet and Health According to God's Will – The Love of Jesus for All Creatures – About the Application of Violence and Bloodshed. The Conversion of a Bird-Catcher – Making Deals with Animals – Moses Did Not Approve Animal Sacrifices …

This book includes a brief autobiography of Gabriele, the prophetess and emissary of God for our time.

1069 pages, softbound, Order No. S007en
ISBN 978-1-890841-38-6, $15.00

You, the Animal –
You, the Human Being
Which Has Higher Values?

A Life with Our
Animal Brothers and Sisters

THE book for animal friends who want to learn more about them. From the contents: Via Scent-Pictures, animals Absorb the Smell of our Sensations, Thoughts and Words and Behave Accordingly – Communication with Animals Through the Input of Messages in Sound and Picture – Why Does an Animal Attack? – The Emergence of Man and of the Earth – Monster Man: Slaughterer, Defiler – Advice for Diet, the Course of the Day, etc.

108 pages, Order No. S133en
ISBN 978-1-890841-25-6, $10.00

The Prophet:
Fundamental Issues of Our Time
to Think About and to serve in
Self-Recognition

Animals Lament –
The Prophet Denounces!
160 pages, Order No. PR015en
ISBN 978-1-890841-43-0, $2.50

The Prophet
The Murder of Animals Is the Death of Humans

60 pages, Order No. PR016en
ISBN 978-1-890841-26-3
$2.50

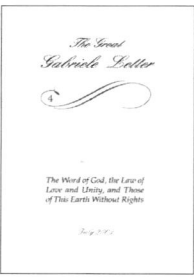

Gabriele Letter No. 4:
The Word of God, the Law of Love and Unity, and Those of This Earth Without Rights

The Gabriele Letters are meant to make alert people aware of how weak in character and schizophrenic our society has become and that the majority of people, thoughtlessly and with dulled senses, accept everything that the upper ranks of society prescribe. Unfortunately, few people practice self-criticism. This is why they cannot view their environment critically and see through those who are literally pulling the wool over their eyes.

168 pages, Order No. GL004en
ISBN 978-1-890841-34-8, $2.50

*We will be happy to send you our catalog
and free brochures*
The Word – The Universal Spirit
P.O. Box 3549
Woodbridge, CT 06525
Order No. 1-800-846-2691

www.Universal-Spirit.org